A NATION CONCEIVED AND DEDICATED

AMERICAN ADVENTURES PROGRAM
VOLUME 1:1620-1860

by

Corinne Hoexter and Ira Peck

Contributing Editors
ROGER FREUDIGMAN
WILLIAM L. DEERING • ARNOLD GOLDSTEIN

Consultants
EDWARD L. BILLER
Supervisor of Social Studies, Baltimore City Schools

JOSEPH LEWBIN
Teacher of Reading and Social Studies,
San Francisco Unified School District

DAVID J. ROTHMAN
Associate Professor of American History,
Columbia University, New York City

Designer
IRMGARD LOCHNER

Photo Editor
MARILYN MOSKOWITZ

SCHOLASTIC BOOK SERVICES
NEW YORK TORONTO LONDON SYDNEY AUCKLAND TOKYO

CONTENTS

PART 1

SEARCH
FOR
FREEDOM

A NEW START

On May 13, 1607, three small ships sailed up a quiet river in Virginia. Four young boys and about 100 men looked out at the woods along the river bank. They had come from England to start a colony here.

The place where they landed had many swamps and muddy pools. But the men liked this spot. Soon they began cutting down trees and building a village. They called it Jamestown, in honor of their King, James I of England. Jamestown was soon hit by hunger, disease, and Indian attacks. But the village went on, and it grew. It was the first English settlement in America that did.

From Jamestown, the colony of Virginia was started. Then, in 1620, more Englishmen landed farther north on the coast of America. This time they came in families, with wives and children. They built a settlement called Plymouth, named after a town in England. From this and other nearby settlements, the colony of Massachusetts grew. Soon more and more Englishmen, and people from many other countries, came to America. By 1733 there were 13 English colonies along the Atlantic coast. They stretched from Georgia in the South to Canada in the North.

America was a wild and rugged land when the first settlers arrived. All of it belonged to the original Americans, the Indians. Many of the Indians were friendly and helpful to the settlers at first. Later they changed. They began to fight to keep their lands.

Why did people come to America from thousands of miles across the ocean? Why did they leave their home countries for a new land they had never seen? Many people in England and other countries of

Europe were poor. In England thousands of farmers had been driven off the land by rich landowners. Many of these country people had become drifters and beggars in the towns. Large numbers of town and city people were also out of work. In America there was plenty of land. If a man who knew farming could just get to America and work very hard, he might own his own farm in a few years. A man who knew a trade might set up a shop in one of the new settlements. America was like a magnet to people who wanted to make a new start in life.

America was also like a magnet to people who wanted more religious freedom. Many people in Europe were badly treated because of their religious beliefs. In England, for example, everyone had to belong to the Church of England. That was the law. But many Englishmen did not like the Church of England. Among them were Quakers, Roman Catholics, and several Protestant groups. Large numbers of these people were willing to cross the Atlantic just so they could worship as they pleased.

English traders and businessmen were glad to see colonies growing up in America. They wanted a market in the New World where English factory products could be sold. And they wanted to buy many of the products of the New World, like furs and wood. Colonies would help to make England rich.

The people from other countries who came to the English colonies were mostly Scotch-Irish, French, German, Dutch, and Swedish. There were colonists from other lands as well. Before long they became quite different from the people in their home countries. As time went by all of the newcomers became more and more "American."

One other group of people began coming to America very early. These were Africans who had been brought to the New World as slaves. For them, America was not a land of freedom or new hope. But they helped America to grow in many ways.

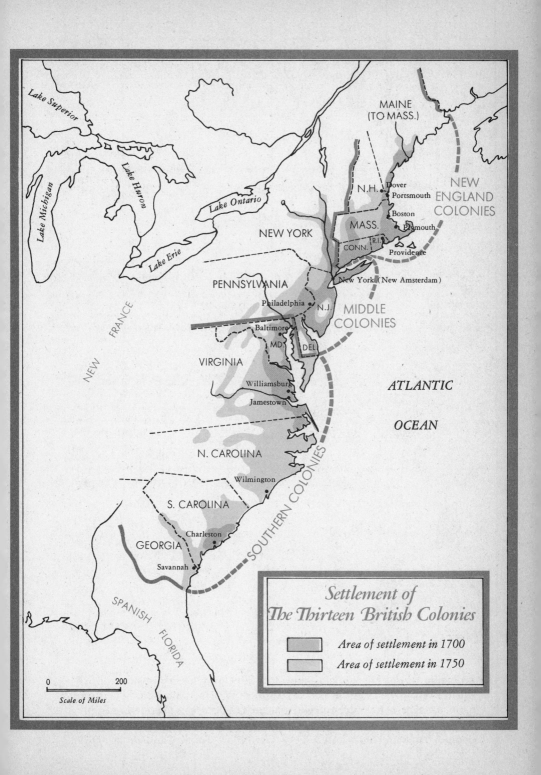

Lake Superior

Lake Michigan

Lake Huron

Lake Ontario

Lake Erie

MAINE
(TO MASS.)

N.H. Dover
Portsmouth

NEW
ENGLAND
COLONIES

Boston

MASS.

Plymouth

NEW YORK

CONN. R.I.

Providence

PENNSYLVANIA

New York (New Amsterdam)

Philadelphia

N.J.

MIDDLE
COLONIES

NEW FRANCE

Baltimore

MD

DEL

VIRGINIA

ATLANTIC

Williamsburg

OCEAN

Jamestown

N. CAROLINA

Wilmington

S. CAROLINA

SOUTHERN COLONIES

GEORGIA

Charleston

Savannah

SPANISH

FLORIDA

0   200

Scale of Miles

Settlement of
The Thirteen British Colonies

Area of settlement in 1700

Area of settlement in 1750

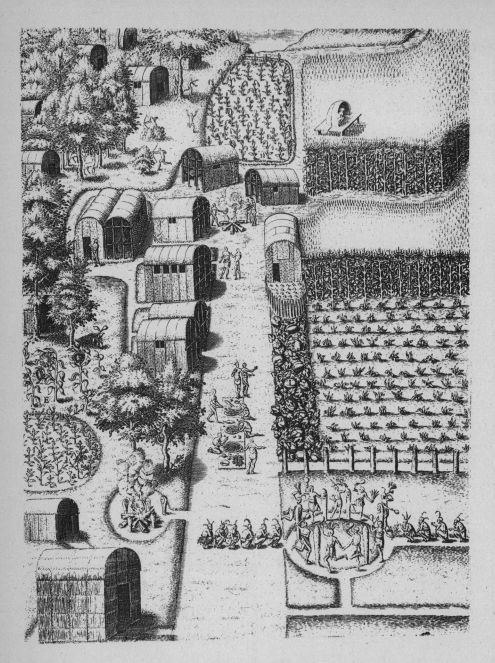

An Indian "towne" in Virginia (above), as drawn by an Englishman in 1587, was clean and well kept. It had a central street lined with bark houses and plantings of corn, tobacco, and watermelon. On the opposite page are English settlements: (upper) Savannah, Georgia, in 1734, one year after settlers cleared the land, and (lower) busy Charleston, South Carolina, in 1739.

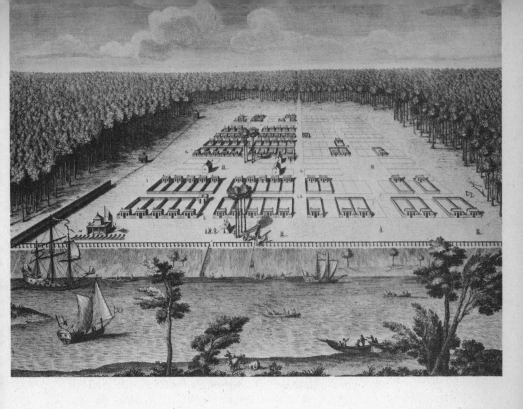

For people seeking religious freedom, America was a magnet. Above: a Puritan church service in early New England. Puritan sermons sometimes took hours. Below: Philadelphia Baptists watch their minister baptize a new member. Upper right: an old English print makes fun of a Quaker meeting. Many Quakers, or Friends, later went to Pennsylvania. Lower right: an offshoot of the Quakers in America were the Shakers, a strict but joyful people named for their trembling, "shaking" dances.

People who came to America brought their skills and know-how with them, as well as their religious beliefs. Ship-building (above) started early in New England, where many people were employed in the codfish industry (below). The page opposite shows a young candle-maker named Benjamin Franklin (upper left), a traveling locksmith (upper right), and a woman working a spinning machine in an early New England cloth factory.

LOCKS OR KEYS.

"Any Locks to repair? Or Keys to be fitted?"

Do you want any Locks
  Put in goodly repair?
Or any Keys fitted,
  To turn true as a hair?

Showing his anger, a colonial barber sends a British officer away with only half a shave. Colonists resented British rule more and more as Britain demanded tax money to pay for colonial defense and upkeep.

On the edge of war. The town of Concord, Massachusetts, is warned of British approach in a painting by Grant Wood, a 20th century artist. Below, British troops entering the Concord of an 18th century artist.

Chapter 1

THEY WERE FREE AT LAST

"Land ho! Land! Land ho!"

The men, women, and children on the little ship looked up. They saw a sailor on top of the tallest mast. He was waving and shouting. They could hardly believe what he was saying. They rushed to the side of the ship. It was true. There was land ahead.

The trip from England had been terrible. They had been at sea for 65 days. Bad storms had shaken and tossed the ship. Great waves had crashed down on it. A big wooden board had cracked and water had poured in. Could the ship go on? Would they have to turn back to England? But somehow the board and the leaks had been fixed. The ship had sailed on.

And now, on November 19, 1620, land was in sight. Many of the people on the ship were sick. All of them were very, very tired. But now they cried with joy and gave thanks to God. At last they could see the shore of the New World.

Who were these people who had made such a dangerous trip? Why had they left their homes to settle in a wilderness?

In England many people had become very unhappy with the national church. "The Church of England has changed too much from the old ways," Roman Catholics said. There were Protestant groups who felt just the opposite. "The Church of England is much too fancy for us," these people said. "We want to follow a simpler way of worship." Most people who felt this way wanted only to "purify" the church, or make it plainer. For this reason they were called Puritans. But others felt that they had to have their own, separate church. These people were called Separatists.

The Separatists were not liked in England. Some of them were thrown in jail. Their church meetings had to be held in secret. Finally a group of Separatists decided to leave England and go to Holland. In Holland most people could worship as they pleased.

Many Separatists packed up and moved to Holland in 1608. They settled in a city called Leyden. The Dutch people made them feel welcome and left them free in church matters. But still the Separatists were not really happy in their new home. Most of them were farm people. They were not used to city life. And as time went on they became unhappy about something else, too — their children were beginning to speak Dutch.

The Separatists wanted to keep their religious freedom. But they also wanted to stay English. Many of them began to think about starting all over again somewhere else — in America. They didn't know much about America. They knew only that it was wild and covered with forests, and that its people were Indians. But they were sure they would be able to get along there.

In July 1620, the first group of Separatists left Holland on a ship named *Speedwell*. They sailed to

Plymouth, England. There they met a second ship, the *Mayflower*, with another group of Separatists. The two ships would leave together for America. The plan was to reach Virginia, where other Englishmen had already set up a colony.

First the two ships were loaded with supplies. Beds, tables, chairs, pots, pans, and axes were put aboard. So were pigs, goats, and chickens. Finally the two ships set out to cross the Atlantic. But the *Speedwell* was in bad shape. When it sprang a leak, both ships had to sail back to England. Everything — people, animals, and supplies — was taken off the *Speedwell* and put aboard the *Mayflower*. Then, on September 16, 1620, the *Mayflower* set out alone for Virginia. It had 102 passengers on board — plus the sailors.

The *Mayflower* was less than 100 feet long. It was too small to steer well in heavy seas. Great storms and gale winds blew it hundreds of miles off course. The land the people saw on November 19, 1620, was nowhere near Virginia. It was Cape Cod, a part of Massachusetts.

Still, the passengers were glad to see land — any land. And they could hardly wait to go ashore. But first they signed a compact, or agreement. They agreed to obey all laws that were made for the good of their settlement. This *Mayflower Compact* marked a big first step toward self-government in the New World.

Then the passengers landed. The first thing the women did was wash all the laundry from more than two months at sea. Groups of men went out to explore. One group set out in a small boat to search for a place to build homes. A group under Captain Miles Standish set out on foot. These men found many Indian graves, and some Indian huts and corn. But they saw no Indians. Then one day they heard a yell. A moment later dozens of arrows flew all around them. Captain Standish ordered his men to fire back with their muskets. Their shots ripped into the trees on all sides. Then they heard another yell, and the

Indians were gone. The woods were silent once more.

After a month of searching, the Englishmen found a good place for a settlement. They named it Plymouth, after the town they had left in England. Here they began chopping down trees with their axes. They split and sawed the trees into thick boards. The English did not build their houses of logs. That was done later on by Swedish settlers, in Delaware.

The first winter in Plymouth was very hard. The settlers had never known such cold in England. About half of them died of hunger and disease. But in the spring, help came. A tall Indian named Samoset walked into the settlement. He was a quiet, helpful man, and so were many of the other Indians who lived in the area. One of them, named Squanto, spoke English very well. He had once been kidnapped by some English sailors, and he had lived nine years in England. When he came back to America, he found that a great sickness had wiped out his tribe.

Squanto came to live in Plymouth. He showed the Englishmen how to plant corn, pumpkins, and beans. He also showed them the Indian ways of hunting and fishing. The Plymouth colony might have died if it had not been for Squanto.

In the fall there was a good harvest. The Englishmen had a big feast to celebrate. And they invited many of their Indian friends to join them. The feast lasted three days. Today we call this feast Thanksgiving. And we call the newcomers "Pilgrims," or wanderers.

The Pilgrims had traveled a long way to find a home where they could worship as they pleased. They had passed through many hardships and dangers. And they knew that there were still many dangers and hardships ahead. Yet not one Pilgrim got aboard the *Mayflower* when it sailed back to England in 1621. They all stayed in their new home in America. Here they had what they wanted. They were free at last.

Chapter 2

SO WISE A RULER

"My prison shall be my grave before I will budge one bit. I owe my conscience to no man."

These words were written in 1668 by a "born fighter" named William Penn. He wrote them while he was in jail in the Tower of London. His cell was a tiny, bare room under the roof. It was icy cold in the winter. In the summer it was steaming hot. Bad prison food made him thin and weak.

Penn didn't have to be in prison. He could have had a soft life. His father was a British navy hero and a rich man. His home was a castle with servants and lots of land.

William Penn's father sent him to the best college in England. Many of the students there were the sons of noblemen. William was friendly and good at sports. He soon became popular.

But after a while, William got into trouble. The law said that all Englishmen had to belong to the Church of England. Puritans and people who belonged to other churches were often beaten up. Sometimes they were put in prison, and even hanged.

William saw many of the college students beat up

Puritans and Separatists and Quakers in the streets. He tried to defend the people who were beaten, and was called a "troublemaker." Penn and some of the other college students stopped going to the Church of England as a protest. Then Penn was kicked out of college.

Penn's father was very angry with him. At first he threw William out of the house. Later he felt sorry and took him back. Then he sent William on a trip to France and Italy to make him a "gentleman."

William did become a gentleman. He wore fine silk clothes and a sword. In London he met the King and many great noblemen. Then in 1665 a terrible disease hit London — the plague, or "black death." Many thousands of people became sick and died. Others ran away from London to save themselves. But the Quakers stayed to take care of the sick and the dying. Penn liked these brave people. Before long, he became a Quaker himself.

What were the Quakers like? They lived simply and wore plain clothes. They did not have churches or regular ministers. They met in plain buildings called "meeting houses." Any member could speak up at meeting when he — or she — felt moved by the spirit of God. The Quakers believed in strict honesty in business. They were against violence and war. They would not serve in the King's army. They were against any kind of unfair treatment of one person by another. They also believed in helping the sick and people in jail. They called themselves "Friends."

William Penn became a leading Quaker. He was thrown into prison in the Tower of London for nine months. He was told to give up his Quaker beliefs. His answer was: "My prison shall be my grave before I will budge one bit." Later Penn was sent to prison two more times.

Penn began to feel that freedom of religion was impossible in England. More and more, he thought of starting a colony in America. In this colony, men and women would be free to worship — and vote — as they pleased.

The King owed Penn's father a lot of money. Penn's father was now dead. So William asked the King to give him, instead of money, a grant of land in America. The King was glad to give Penn some land — anything to get rid of this Quaker trouble-maker. He gave Penn the land that is now Pennsylvania. The name means "Penn's woods."

In 1681 Quakers from England and other countries set sail for Pennsylvania. Penn wrote a *Charter of Liberties* for the new colony. Many years later, it became a model for the U.S. Constitution. The Charter said: the lawmakers of the colony would be elected by the citizens of the colony; every male citizen of the colony could vote; there would be freedom of religion for all; there would be freedom of speech for all; there would be trial by jury for anyone accused of a crime.

Thomas Jefferson, who wrote the Declaration of Independence in 1776, called Penn "the greatest lawgiver the world has produced."

Penn was also a good friend to the Indians of Pennsylvania. He was always honest and fair, and the Indians respected him for it. Penn once told a group of Indians: "All will be brotherhood and love. I consider us all the same flesh and blood, joined by one heart."

An Indian chief replied to this by saying: "The Indians and colonists must live in love as long as the sun and moon give light."

One writer said: "It was the only treaty between Indians and Christians that was never broken."

Penn made Pennsylvania "a free colony for all mankind." It was free not just for Englishmen or Quakers, but for men of all nations and religious beliefs. One colonist said this about Penn: "He is loved and praised by all. The people have never seen so wise a ruler."

Chapter 3

LIBERTY ON TRIAL

Governor William Cosby of New York was angry —
very angry. How dare this newspaper make fun of
him? How dare it say he had cheated people to get
rich? *Nobody* could say that about him. He was never
so insulted in all his life. Well, he wouldn't stand for
it. No, sir. He would stop it right away.

What was all the fuss about?

William Cosby had come to New York from
England in 1732. George II, the King of England,
had made him the governor of the colony. The people
of New York knew very little about Cosby. At first
he seemed all right. He gave big parties, with lots of
good food and wine for everyone. Cosby must have
plenty of money, people said. He wouldn't steal from
them, like some governors had.

But before long, most people in New York changed
their minds about Cosby. He had tried to take a lot
of money from a leading citizen. He was mixed up in

some shady deals to get rich. And he was breaking many rules as governor. Some people in New York wanted to fight against Cosby. They felt that the best way to do it was to start a newspaper that would "show him up." (There was only one newspaper in New York at that time. And it was *for* Cosby.)

The man who was hired to print a second newspaper was Peter Zenger. Zenger had been born in Germany. He came to New York with his mother when he was 13. He learned the printing trade and later started his own printing shop. Zenger did not like Cosby, and he was not afraid to print the truth. He agreed to print a newspaper that would fight Cosby.

The men who wrote for this paper did not sign their real names to their articles. It was too dangerous. The only one who used his real name in the paper was Zenger. He was listed as the printer.

Soon Governor Cosby became very angry with this newspaper. He ordered some copies of it to be burned in the street. Then he ordered the arrest of Peter Zenger. He couldn't arrest the other men because he didn't know their names.

Zenger was thrown into jail. At first he was not allowed to see anyone. Later the judge allowed Zenger to talk to his wife and others through a hole in the door. Zenger's wife was able to print the paper all the time Zenger was in jail. Zenger was questioned night and day. Who wrote the articles for his newspaper? Who paid the money for printing it? Zenger was firm. He would not give the names of his friends.

Zenger spent almost nine months in jail before he got a trial. The charge against him was that he had printed "lies" about Governor Cosby. These "lies" had made the governor look very bad. Zenger's lawyer was a young man. The judges were friends of Cosby. It was almost certain that Zenger would be found guilty.

Just then an old man stood up in court. He was

dressed in fine clothes and wore a fancy wig. "May it please Your Honor," he said to the chief judge, "I am here on the part of Mr. Zenger."

The judge could hardly believe his eyes. This was Andrew Hamilton, one of the greatest lawyers in all the colonies. Was he really going to defend a poor printer against Governor Cosby?

That was exactly what Hamilton was going to do. He had come all the way from Philadelphia to defend Zenger. It was a long trip in those days, and Hamilton was 80 years old.

Now Hamilton began to speak. His voice was strong. He did not deny that Zenger had printed articles against Cosby. But, he said, the government's lawyer had to prove that the articles were not true. If the articles were true, Hamilton said, then Zenger was not guilty of anything.

The government's lawyer became angry. He shouted and got red in the face. But he knew he couldn't prove that the articles were not true.

Hamilton was not finished yet. He told the jury that it was not just Peter Zenger, a poor printer, who was on trial. He said that "the cause of liberty" was on trial. The case was really about "the liberty of speaking and writing truth." He asked the jury to find Zenger not guilty. He said, "Every man who prefers freedom to slavery will honor you."

The jury found Zenger "not guilty." The people in the courtroom cheered loudly.

The next day, Hamilton started back to Philadelphia. Ships in the harbor of New York fired cannons in his honor. It was their way of thanking him for his defense of liberty.

After the Zenger trial, lawmakers in the colonies had to think twice before trying to stop a newspaper from printing the truth. Freedom of the press later became an important part of the Bill of Rights in the U.S. Constitution. Peter Zenger and Andrew Hamilton had shown the way.

Chapter 4

IF THIS BE TREASON

He was a lazy, good-for-nothing kid. That's what everyone said about young Patrick Henry. It was a waste of time sending him to school. He didn't learn anything. All he wanted to do was go fishing or hunt in the woods. Patrick's father, a Virginia farmer, didn't know what to do with the boy. Sometimes he whipped him. Other times he prayed for him. But nothing seemed to help.

Finally Patrick's father took him out of school. It was a happy day for both Patrick and his teachers. At home Patrick's father taught him the Bible, math, and Latin. Patrick really wasn't stupid. He could learn — when he wanted to. The trouble was he did not like school. He liked running around in the woods much more.

Patrick's father worried about the boy. How would he ever earn a living? The older Henry decided to start his son in business. When Patrick was 16, his father bought him a country store. It sold everything from sugar to hairpins. But Patrick was no business-man. On nice days, he would just close the store and go hunting. There were lots of wild animals in the forests of Virginia in those days. (It was then 1751.) And Patrick knew how to use a rifle. After a while, Patrick's father had to close up the store for good.

At 18 Patrick fell in love with a poor farmer's daughter and married her. Now he tried to make a living as a tobacco farmer. But he had no luck at farming and soon had to give it up. Then he started another store. But he had to close this one, too.

By this time, Patrick Henry had three children as well as a wife to support. He knew he had to make

29

a living in *some* way. There was one thing he did well — he was a very good speaker. So he decided to become a lawyer. He studied law books night and day for six weeks. Then he took a test and passed. At 24 Patrick Henry became a lawyer.

Henry's gift for speaking helped him win many cases. His first really big case came up when he was 27. It had started out as an argument between the Virginia legislature and some church ministers. Virginia at that time had a church supported by public taxes. Many people thought that the ministers of this church were overpaid. So the Virginia legislature passed a law that cut the ministers' salaries.

The ministers were angry about this. When King George III heard about it, he was angry, too. He threw out the Virginia legislature's new law. Then the ministers went to court. They wanted all the money they had lost since their pay had been cut.

This was where lawyer Henry stepped into the case. He stood for the idea that Virginia didn't owe any back pay to the ministers. Nobody thought he would win. What jury would dare go against the King? But when Henry got up to speak, there was "magic" in his voice. He said to the jury:

What right did the King of England have to throw out a law passed by the people of Virginia? The voice of the people, Henry said, is the voice of God. When a king throws out a law passed by the people, the people do not have to obey him any more.

This was pretty strong talk in those days, when kings were very powerful. Some people in the courtroom were shocked. But Patrick Henry won his case.

The young lawyer was now a hero in Virginia. He was especially a hero to the small farmers and the woodsmen. They elected him to the Virginia legislature. Soon after, Henry really gave the people of Virginia something to talk about.

King George had put a stamp tax on "every piece of paper" used in the American colonies. This meant that any business paper or legal paper had to have a stamp on it. Even a marriage license wouldn't be any good unless it had a stamp on it. Many Americans were angry about this. They didn't want to pay for a stamp every time they signed something. Besides, they believed that only their own legislatures had the right to tax them. But few people were brave enough to protest out loud.

Then, on May 29, 1765, Patrick Henry got up to speak in the Virginia legislature. The stamp tax was against the law, he said. Under the law, the people could be taxed only by their own representatives. The colonists had no representatives in the British government. So how could the British government place a stamp tax on the colonists? It couldn't, Henry said — unless it broke the law.

Henry said that nobody in Virginia should obey the stamp tax law. Then he really shocked everybody. He compared King George to a *tyrant* — a ruler who breaks the law and becomes an enemy of his people. And he warned the King that tyrants were sometimes killed.

Suddenly there were shouts of "Treason! Treason!" from those who were loyal to the King. Henry waited until the shouting died down. Then he said, *"If this be treason, make the most of it!"*

Word of Henry's speech traveled fast. Before long, Americans in all the colonies refused to pay the stamp tax. Sometimes they burned stamps and beat up the tax collectors. In Boston there were riots against the taxes.

Did the British learn anything from the uproar over the stamp tax? Some people thought so. The British took back, or repealed, the stamp tax law in 1766. But at the same time they passed another law — the Declaratory Act. This act said that Britain had full power to make laws for the colonies and people of America — "in all cases whatsoever."

These were fighting words.

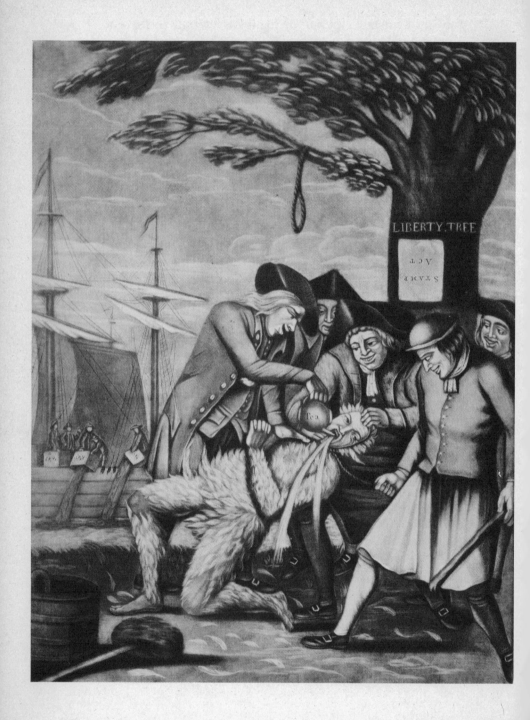

Chapter 5

BLOOD ON THE SNOW

It was a cold winter night in Boston. The moon was shining brightly over the snowy streets. On one street, a lone British soldier stood guard. Suddenly an icy snowball flew past his ear. Another nearly knocked his hat off. A third caught him right on the chest. The snowballs were thrown by a group of boys across the street. Soon the boys began to yell at the soldier. "Lobster back! Bloody back!" they shouted. British soldiers wore red uniforms in those days. Americans often called them "redcoats" or "lobster backs."

There had been many fights between British soldiers and Boston people. What were the fights about? The British had backed up their Declaratory Act. They had placed several new taxes on the colonies. The people hated these taxes. In Boston there were riots against them. The people hated many of the other laws made for them in far-off England. "Why should we obey these laws?" many colonists asked. "We had no part in making them."

King George III of Britain became angry. In 1768 he sent 4,000 soldiers to Boston to stop the riots. The people of Boston hated these soldiers even more than the taxes. They had to make room for the soldiers in inns, taverns, and other privately owned buildings.

Some of the soldiers were put up in people's homes. And that wasn't all. Many of the soldiers took off-duty jobs that the colonists themselves needed. Tough dock workers often attacked soldiers who were off duty.

On this night, March 5, 1770, the lone British guard was nervous. A number of men and women had joined the shouting boys. Soon there was a large crowd. The soldier then fixed his bayonet on his rifle. The crowd nearly went wild. "Kill him! Kill him!" they screamed. A bunch of dock workers and sailors joined the crowd. One of them was a giant of a man named Crispus Attucks. He was part black, part Indian, and part white.

The British guard called for help. Seven redcoats led by a captain came to his aid. The captain told his men to load their rifles, but he ordered them *not* to fire. Soon the crowd began getting out of hand. A British guard was knocked down. Suddenly someone shouted "Fire!" No one ever found out who shouted it. But the British soldiers began shooting.

When the smoke cleared, Attucks and two other men were dead. Two more lay dying in the snow. This was the "Boston Massacre."

The angry crowd charged forward again. Soon other soldiers turned out to halt the rioters. War against Britain might have started right then and there. But Governor Thomas Hutchinson of Massachusetts rushed to the scene and made a speech to quiet the crowd. He promised the people that the soldiers would be put on trial.

The next day a Boston leader named Samuel Adams spoke out. He said the "redcoat butchers" had to be punished. But others felt that the crowd was partly to blame for the "massacre."

A cousin of Samuel Adams, John Adams, agreed to defend the soldiers in a court trial. John Adams was an excellent lawyer. (He would one day become President of the United States.) As a result of the trial, the British captain and six of his men were freed. Two others got mild punishment. They were branded on the thumb with a hot iron.

But Samuel Adams kept making speeches about the bloody "massacre" and the courage of the men who were killed. Before long many people were thinking of Attucks and his friends as heroes and great patriots — lovers of their country. And they were thinking of the British as murderers — and enemies.

PART 2

BREAKING AWAY

THE ROAD TO REVOLUTION

Britain and France fought a long, hard war between 1754 and 1763. In North America it was called the French and Indian War. Here the French and their Indian allies battled against the British and the American colonists. The British and Americans finally won the war. France had to give Canada and all of its other lands on the North American continent to Britain.

Britain had won a huge piece of land in North America. But the war had cost a huge amount of money. Most British leaders thought that the American colonies should start paying taxes to cover part of the cost. They also thought it was time the colonies began to obey some of the British laws on trade.

These laws were meant to hold back the colonies' trade with France, Holland, and other countries. The laws also said the colonies could not trade with each other in certain products. Only British factories could sell their goods in all the colonies. Why? Because Britain wanted the colonies to trade mainly with Britain. And it wanted the colonies to produce only those things that Britain needed. After all, the British thought, that was what colonies were for.

The colonists did not like these trade laws. They had not obeyed them for a long time. Many American merchants had become rich by smuggling — carrying on trade that was against these laws. The British knew perfectly well that the colonists were smuggling. But nobody had ever tried very hard to stop it. "So what if the colonists smuggle a bit," some British leaders said. "If the colonists get rich, they will buy more goods from Britain."

But now the British government decided to send soldiers and ships to the colonies. They would not only protect the colonies. They would also back up the trade laws. That way the colonists themselves would pay for part of the upkeep of the soldiers and ships. Taxpayers in Britain liked this idea. They were tired of paying all the bills for America.

The Americans did not like these British plans. They did not see why British soldiers had to be kept on American soil. The French had been beaten. What need was there for British soldiers now? Besides, many traders and businessmen in the colonies would lose money if Britain backed up the trade laws.

Most colonists at this time still thought of the British King as their King. But they didn't think of the British government, or Parliament, as their government. Certainly not when it came to taxes. "By what right does Britain's Parliament pass tax laws for us?" the colonists asked. "We don't have any representatives in Parliament. Our representatives are right here in our own legislatures. So only our own legislatures can tax us."

Parliament made the colonists angry in another way. It said that none of them could settle on land west of the Appalachian Mountains. This was Indian country, and Parliament did not want to spend money on any more wars with the Indians. If the colonists kept out of the Indian area, there would be no more trouble. But the Americans felt they had a right to settle on this land.

The colonists struck back at Britain in many ways. Their best weapon was the boycott — refusing to buy British goods. Boycotts made the British take back all the new taxes except for a small one on tea.

But even this tax made the colonists angry. "Parliament has no right to make us pay *any* such tax," they said. Some colonial leaders began forming groups called the Sons of Liberty. Sons of Liberty "clubs" sprang up in several colonies. They led a protest movement against taxes. Some of their members also led violent attacks against tax collectors — and sometimes even soldiers.

Some colonists began to prepare for a showdown with the British. It began on April 19, 1775. That day, about 700 British soldiers left Boston and marched on Concord, Massachusetts. They wanted to seize the guns and gunpowder the colonists had stored there — just in case. At Lexington, along the way to Concord, some of the colonists tried to stop the British. Shots were fired on both sides. This was the beginning of the American Revolution.

Many people thought that the colonies had very little chance of winning a war against Britain. Britain had one of the best armies in Europe. The colonies started out with small groups of militia — part-time fighters who trained for only a few days each year. Britain had the largest navy in the world. The colonies had no warships. Britain also had many factories that could turn out war supplies. The colonies had very few.

Britain had five times as many men as the colonies. It had a strong government and plenty of money to hire foreign soldiers with. The Americans had a central government so weak it had to beg for money.

Not all Americans were in favor of this war. Many of them gave no help to either side. About one out of three stayed loyal to Britain. They called themselves Loyalists. But the American patriots called them *Tories*. Many Loyalists — or Tories — fought alongside the British in the war. This made the Revolutionary War also a civil war, because some Americans fought against other Americans.

But the American patriots had some strong points working in their favor. They were fighting on their own land. They were fighting for a cause they believed in. For the British, the war was thousands of miles from home. Many of their soldiers were fighting only for pay, not a cause like freedom. The Americans knew how to fight Indian-style, too. Many of them had woodsmen's rifles. These were better than British muskets.

America could not have won the war without foreign help. Most of it came from France. Even more important, the Americans could not have won without a leader like General George Washington.

Washington took no pay as commander-in-chief of the American forces. Yet he worked day and night with these forces. He molded them into a Continental Army. He led this army for eight long years. He led it through summer heat and bitter winter cold. He stayed with his job through victory and defeat. And there were many defeats. His great courage and self-control were an example to others. Washington was a man who could get other men to follow him. He got men to drill and to fight and to sign up for new terms of service — even when they had to wait for their pay. Sometimes his men did not know if they would be paid at all.

The Americans had other great fighters for their cause, too. Some were little known men like Haym Salomon, a Jewish businessman who gave all his money to the war effort. Some were well known leaders such as Benjamin Franklin and Thomas Jefferson. Others were men who left their homes in Europe to help the American cause. Friedrich von Steuben, a German, trained many of Washington's troops. Thaddeus Kosciusko, from Poland, drew up American defense plans at Saratoga and West Point. The Marquis de Lafayette came from France at the age of 19. He became a major general in the Continental Army. Washington thought of him almost as a son.

Without the great cause of freedom to believe in, the Americans could not have fought on for so long. Without such heroes to fight for this cause, the Americans could not have won the war.

THE HORSE AMERICA, *throwing his Master.*

Two views of colonial strength: a British cartoon shows King George III being thrown by his horse "America." Below, an American cartoon tells colonists to forget differences and unite against their enemy.

JOIN, or DIE.

George Washington, commander in chief of all the American forces during the Revolutionary War, shown here in his general's uniform during a peaceful moment. Washington was a quiet and dignified man who knew how to command the respect and loyalty of other soldiers — even when the going was hardest and it looked as if all were lost.

Above: Americans sometimes fought the British "Indian-style" — from the cover of rocks and trees, instead of out in the open. Below: Washington leads Americans in a surprise attack on the British at Princeton, N.J.

Two who came from Europe to help the American cause were Thaddeus
Kosciusko (above) of Poland and Friedrich von Steuben of Germany.

One of Washington's most trusted and able helpers was the young Marquis de Lafayette, who sailed from France at 19 to serve as a volunteer in America. He was soon made a major general in Washington's army.

Chapter 6

TEA, TAXES, AND TROUBLE

Three ships with a dangerous cargo were anchored in Boston Harbor. The cargo was a shipment of tea. But it might as well have been gunpowder. No one dared to unload it. What were they afraid of?

The tea had a British tax on it. Samuel Adams and other colonial leaders had spoken out against such a tax. Adams said the tea must not be unloaded. He asked Governor Thomas Hutchinson of Massachusetts to send the ships back to England. Hutchinson refused to do so.

Now it was the night of December 16, 1773. It was damp and cold. Governor Hutchinson was in his country house outside of Boston. He was worried.

"The ships must be unloaded by tomorrow," he told a friend. "I'll never send that tea back to England."

"I'm afraid no one is brave enough to touch that tea," answered his friend. "Those outlaws, the Sons of Liberty, are ready with tar and feathers. They'll use it on anyone who tries to unload those ships."

Just then there was a knock at the door. A wet and tired messenger came in.

"I come from a meeting in Boston," he said. "The people there beg you to send back the tea."

"The ships will never leave Boston with the tea on board," said Governor Hutchinson. "The King's laws must be obeyed."

In Boston a large crowd of people waited for the messenger to return. They were angry. They had been listening to many speeches against British taxes. "Whoever drinks tea is a traitor!" they shouted. "We will not sell our rights for tea leaves!"

Just then the messenger returned. He rushed up to Samuel Adams with Governor Hutchinson's answer. Adams was on the speaker's platform. He turned and told the meeting, "The ships stay. This meeting can do nothing further to save the country!"

A moment later wild war cries were heard outside. A troop of 150 Boston men was parading in the street. They were made up to look like Indians. They carried clubs, tomahawks, and knives. "Make Boston Harbor a teapot tonight!" they shouted.

The "Indians" rowed out into the harbor. On the dock a big crowd of people cheered them. The "Indians" then boarded the tea ships. The British sailors did not try to fight them. Soon the "Indians" were dumping big chests of tea into the harbor. When they finished, they lined up on the dock like soldiers and marched away. No British soldier made a move to stop them.

The news of the Boston "tea party" shocked England. Many Americans were shocked by it too. King George III was not only shocked. He was filled with rage. He ordered the port of Boston closed. He sent more soldiers there to keep it closed. No ships could enter or leave the port.

But people in the other colonies came to the help of Boston. They sent money and food and supplies. The colonies were beginning to unite against England. They were beginning to think of the mother country as an enemy.

Chapter 7

FATHER OF LIBERTY

"Quick! Wake up Mr. Adams and Mr. Hancock. The British are coming!"

It was Paul Revere talking. He had just made his famous "midnight ride" from Boston to Lexington. "The British are coming!" he had warned the people along the way.

What did the British want? They were out to grab the guns and gunpowder stored by the "Minutemen" in Concord. The Minutemen were farmers who were training to fight the British if war came. The British also wanted to arrest John Hancock and Samuel Adams, who were staying in Lexington. Hancock and Adams had been stirring up the people against British rule. That had not been a hard thing to do after the King ordered the port of Boston closed.

Soon Hancock and Adams came downstairs. "You must leave at once for Philadelphia," Revere told them. "The British want to send you to London — to hang you as criminals. Redcoats are on their way here right now."

Hancock was easily excited. At first he didn't want to leave. He and Adams had an argument about it. Finally Adams told Hancock it would be foolish for him to stay. Hancock was too important to let himself be captured.

It was dawn when Adams and Hancock drove away in Hancock's carriage. Suddenly shots were heard coming from Lexington. British soldiers and Minutemen were firing at each other. It was the beginning of the American Revolution. The date was April 19, 1775.

John Hancock was 38. He was a rich merchant and had fine clothes and manners. Samuel Adams was 53. He was a poor man and looked much older than his age. His head sometimes shook. His voice was not always strong. Yet, more than any other man, Adams had fanned the flames of rebellion against the British. He was known as the man the British most wanted to hang.

Samuel Adams was born in Boston in 1722. He was the son of a brewer who had done very well in business. But when Samuel Adams went into business, he failed. He owed lots of money. His children often wore clothes given to them by friends.

Soon Adams turned from business to politics. At

politics he was a master. He was elected to the Massachusetts legislature. He fought hard against British taxes. He was a leader of the Boston men who called themselves the Sons of Liberty. They tarred and feathered tax collectors and stirred up riots against the British. Adams attacked British rule every chance he got. His speeches and writings whipped up the anger of the people of Boston. After the Boston "massacre," there were angry people in all the colonies. Later Adams gave the signal for the "Indian raid" on the tea ships in Boston Harbor.

King George III closed the port of Boston after the "tea party." The city's trade and shipping were brought to a stop. Then Adams called for a meeting of the leaders of all the colonies. This became the First Continental Congress. It met in Philadelphia in 1774. The angry colonial leaders sent the King a long list of complaints. The King paid no attention to them. Meanwhile the Minutemen began to train.

On the night and morning of April 18–19, 1775, the redcoats marched on Lexington and Concord. They burned whatever ammunition they could find. Then they ran into the Minutemen. On the march back to Boston, 273 British soldiers fell dead or wounded. The Minutemen fired on them "Indian-style" — from the cover of trees, walls, and houses.

Warned by Paul Revere, Adams and Hancock were already on their way to Philadelphia. By the time they arrived, the Continental Congress had been called into session again. Adams gave some fiery speeches before the members of the Congress. He called for liberty for the American colonies. A little more than a year later, the Declaration of Independence was signed. Then Adams' main job was done — he had given his countrymen the courage to stand up and fight for their rights.

Samuel Adams died in 1803 at the age of 81. Patriots in America have honored him ever since as "the father of liberty."

Chapter 8

A COSTLY VICTORY AT BUNKER HILL

"Don't fire until you see the whites of their eyes!"

This famous order was given by the American commander at the bloody Battle of Bunker Hill. It was the first big battle of the Revolutionary War.

How did it come about? Boston was in the hands of the British. But across the river to the north were two hills. They were called Bunker Hill and Breed's Hill. If the Americans put guns on those hills, they could fire down on Boston and the British warships in the harbor. This might force the British to leave the city. The British decided to take the hills.

The Americans heard of the British plan. They sent about 1,000 soldiers to build a dirt and wood fort on Bunker Hill. They built it in a great hurry on the night of June 16, 1775. And for some reason that has never been explained, they built it on Breed's Hill instead of Bunker Hill. But the fight that was fought there has gone down in history as the Battle of Bunker Hill.

Early the next morning, British warships opened fire on the Americans. They did little damage, but the noise and smoke was frightening. Colonel William Prescott, the American commander, drove his men hard to finish the fort.

At 1:30 in the afternoon, barges began carrying British soldiers across the river. Their tall helmets and bayonets gleamed in the sun. They were among

the finest and best-dressed soldiers in all of Europe.

British General William Howe had a simple plan. One group of redcoats would attack the hill from the front. Another group would circle it on the right, and attack from the rear.

The main British lines marched up the hill. Nothing happened at first. Colonel Prescott had given his famous "whites of their eyes" order. The British came up higher and higher. Suddenly a voice at the top shouted, "Fire!" A blaze of flame and smoke ripped the British lines. The redcoats tried to fire back, but they were cut down again and again. Finally they could stand it no longer. They turned and ran back to safety.

The Americans thought victory was theirs. But 15 minutes later General Howe ordered another attack on the hill. This time the redcoats had to climb over the bodies of their comrades. Again the redcoats were met by deadly fire. For the second time they fell back in disorder.

Still the British did not give up. Once more they formed their lines for an attack on the hill. By now the Americans were short of gunpowder and bullets. Even so they sent a heavy fire into the British. This time the British did not turn and run. Though many were killed, they shouted, "Push on! Push on!" One of the British soldiers who fell was Major John Pitcairn. He had fought at Lexington and Concord. He was killed by a bullet fired by Salem Prince, a free Negro.

Soon the redcoats climbed over the walls of the fort. Inside, British and Americans fought hand-to-hand. Finally Colonel Prescott ordered the Americans to retreat.

The British had captured Breed's Hill — but nearly half their men were dead or wounded. It was a costly victory. One British general said, "Another such victory would have ruined us." Both sides now knew they had a hard and bloody struggle on their hands.

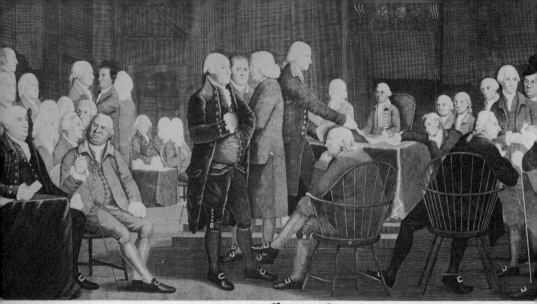

Chapter 9

A DANGEROUS
DECLARATION

"We ... do ... declare that these United Colonies are, and of Right ought to be Free and Independent States."

These words are part of America's Declaration of Independence. They were dangerous words at the time they were written. It was June 1776, and the colonies had been in rebellion against Britain for a little over a year. The Americans had won some victories in this struggle. But so had the British. It was much too early to know which side would win.

Many Americans were not really sure yet just what they were fighting for. Were they fighting to make Britain take back its unfair taxes? Were they fighting for the right to make their own laws? Were they fighting to throw off *all* British rule — to be free and independent?

American patriot leaders had been arguing this question for months. Many of them had been meeting in Philadelphia almost since the fighting had started. This meeting was the Second Continental Congress.

Most of the members of the Congress were strongly in favor of independence. Even some who had been against it at first had later changed their minds. By this time, several battles had been fought. Many American lives had been lost. It now seemed as if independence was the only goal that would make this fighting and bloodshed worthwhile.

But there were still some members of the Congress who were against declaring independence. They felt that too many Americans were still loyal to the King. And a declaration of independence would turn the rebellion against Britain into an all-out war. They felt that the colonies were too weak to win an all-out war.

There were many arguments on both sides. But while the arguments were still going on, a group of men was chosen to write a Declaration of Independence. The group gave the main job of writing the Declaration to one man, Thomas Jefferson of Virginia. Jefferson was then 33 years old, the second youngest member of the Congress.

Jefferson knew that a Declaration of Independence was dangerous — especially while some of the colonies were still against it. But he also knew that some of the colonies were not willing to wait any longer. They might declare independence on their own, even if others held back. Jefferson must have remembered something Benjamin Franklin had said:

"We must all hang together, for if we don't, we'll all hang separately."

Jefferson felt that a great change had come over America since the fighting had started. Men no longer drank to King George's health in taverns. Instead they talked about a little book written by Tom Paine. Paine was an Englishman who had been in America for only a short time. In his book, *Common Sense*, Paine called King George "the royal brute of Britain." He said it made no sense for Americans to bow to a tyrant. Across the last page of *Common Sense* were the daring words, "The Free and Independent States of America."

Paine's book had been bought and read by thousands. Jefferson himself had read it, and he agreed with what it said. Sentence by sentence, Jefferson began writing his Declaration of Independence.

By July 1, 1776, the Continental Congress was listening to the last arguments on the question: Should it take a stand for independence? Should it hold back?

The arguments went on for nine hours. By this time, no one was against the idea that the 13 colonies should be independent. But some members were against *declaring* independence. They said it was too early. One member said it would be "like destroying our house in winter, before we have got another shelter."

Other members gave strong speeches in favor of declaring independence. They pointed out that Britain had made no move to take away any of the causes of the fighting. Instead Britain had sent more ships and troops to the colonies to crush the Americans by force. The King had never sent an answer to the long list of complaints that the First Continental Congress drew up. Then the Second Congress sent him another list of complaints. It also tried to explain to the King all the reasons why the colonists had taken up arms against his troops. It sent the King a "Declaration of the Causes and Necessity of Taking Up Arms." But again the King had sent no answer. Instead he issued a statement saying that the colonies were "in rebellion."

Now the fighting had been going on for more than a year. Those in favor of independence argued that the fighting was no longer a "rebellion" against Britain's unfair laws. It had changed into an all-out *revolution* against the government itself — a fight for complete separation and independence from it. One member said that this change had already taken place "in the hearts and minds of the people." How could the Congress hold back? Wasn't it supposed to be *leading* the people?

The Congress met early the next day, July 2, to take its vote. It came out strongly in favor of declaring independence. Every member knew that this was one of the most important decisions ever made. Now the true goal of the fight against Britain had been set.

Many thought that July 2 — the date of the vote for independence — would go down in history as America's Independence Day. But that was not to be.

For the rest of July 2, and on July 3 and 4, the Congress looked over the Declaration of Independence that Thomas Jefferson had written. Was this the Declaration the Congress should adopt? Many members asked for changes here and there. About one quarter of the writing was scratched out. But in the end, most of Jefferson's Declaration was left almost as he had written it.

July 4 was a hot day. The members of the Congress wiped their foreheads with their handkerchiefs. One by one they voted "Yes" to Jefferson's Declaration. Then the Declaration was sent, scratches and all, to a nearby printing house to be printed. July 4, the day Jefferson's Declaration was approved, has been celebrated as Independence Day in the United States ever since.

Soon the Declaration appeared in all the newspapers. Now, at last, Americans understood what they were fighting for. Now the "United Colonies" of America were the United *States* of America. Americans were no longer the "subjects" of a faraway King, but *citizens* of a nation of their own.

The Declaration's words are still fresh today:

"We hold these truths to be self-evident, that all men are created equal, that they are endowed by their Creator with certain . . . Rights, that among these are Life, Liberty, and the pursuit of Happiness. . . ."

Chapter 10

A NEEDED VICTORY

It looked like the end for General George Washington's army. Unless he got more men, he said, "the game will be pretty near up."

Washington and his army had been driven off Long Island and out of New York. They had fallen back across New Jersey. Then the British had chased the Americans across the Delaware River into Pennsylvania. It was now December 1776. Washington had less than 3,000 men left out of about 20,000. The rest had either been killed, taken prisoner, or had deserted. Many American soldiers had no shoes, shirts, or coats. Winter was closing in and the men were freezing. At the end of the year, their terms of service would be up. Then most of them would leave the army and go home. Washington badly needed a victory just to hold his army together.

Across the Delaware River, in Trenton, New Jersey, were 1,500 enemy soldiers. Their home was the small German state of Hesse, and they were called Hessians. They were hired by the British. They had chased Washington's army across New Jersey. Now they were enjoying their victory and the coming of Christmas.

Washington sent a spy, John Honeyman, among the Hessians. Honeyman told Washington that the Hessians were planning a big party on Christmas. There would be lots of eating — and drinking. The Hessians would be in no condition to fight.

This was the chance Washington needed. He planned an attack on the Hessians. "Victory or death!" Washington said.

On the night of December 25, Washington's men began to cross the Delaware. They used 40-foot rowboats. The river was flooded and full of ice. Huge chunks of ice crashed against the boats. But somehow 2,000 men and 18 cannons were rowed across. The men split up into two columns and headed for Trenton, nine miles away. One column took the river road. The other took an inland road. Snow, sleet, and hail fell upon the soldiers.

Both roads to Trenton were covered with ice and snow. Men slipped and fell along the way. Men in bare feet or torn shoes made a trail of blood on the snowy roads.

About 7:30 a.m., a sleepy Hessian guard thought he saw men moving on the inland road. He called out a warning — too late. Shots rang out, men ran and shouted. Down by the river, the second column of Americans was charging with bayonets. Cannons began to open fire.

Colonel Johann Rall, the Hessian commander, was awakened by the noise. He was still dazed from the Christmas party. Probably he had a bad hangover. But he dashed bravely into the streets between the stone barracks. He cursed and called his sleepy, tired men out to fight. Most of them couldn't even get into action. The American rifle and cannon fire was too heavy.

Finally Colonel Rall was hit by a bullet and fell wounded. The frightened Hessians threw down their rifles and surrendered. Rall died after giving up to Washington. More than 1,000 of the enemy were taken prisoner. Only two of Washington's men were killed and three were wounded.

The Americans were amazed by their victory. They wore rags — but they had beaten a tough, trained army. As a result, many Americans signed up for more service. Washington's army was saved. It would fight on until help came from France.

Chapter 11

THE DEFEAT OF GENTLEMAN JOHNNY

"Gentleman Johnny" Burgoyne rode among his British troops, calling on them to fight. American bullets ripped his coat. He laughed and waved his hat. His men cheered — and died. This was part of the Battle of Saratoga. It ended in a bloody British defeat. This defeat was the turning point of the Revolutionary War.

How did it happen? General Burgoyne had a plan. It was to cut off New England from the rest of the American colonies. To do this, he would lead an army down from Canada and take Albany, New York. Then he would march down the Hudson River Valley and join forces with the British in New York City. With the Hudson under British control, the Americans would not be able to get supplies from New England. Burgoyne started out in June 1777 with more than 7,000 men.

At first his plan seemed to go well. Burgoyne's army easily captured Fort Ticonderoga, New York. But soon Burgoyne ran into trouble. His army had to cut its way through thick forests. It had to cross swamps and streams. It had to build some 40 bridges along the way. His men became weak and sick. Then some of his Indian allies scalped an American woman. Many Americans in New York who had been for the British now turned against them.

Then Burgoyne made a bad mistake. He sent about 700 of his Hessian soldiers to Vermont to grab food and horses for his men. At Bennington they were attacked by untrained American soldiers. Almost all of the Hessians were killed or captured. Many of the soldiers sent to help them were also lost. In all Burgoyne lost about 900 men.

On September 19, Burgoyne's army met a larger American army near Saratoga. The British marched out of a forest into an open field. Up ahead men with fur caps and long rifles lay in wait, hidden among the trees. Suddenly there was the crack of American rifles. Their main targets were British officers. Many were killed. British gunners were picked off before they could load their cannons.

The British fled back to the woods. When the Americans charged them, the British drove them back. For three hours the two armies fought back and forth across a field. The Americans finally pulled back, but the British had lost more than 600 men.

Burgoyne waited for help but none came. Then, on October 7, the two armies fought it out again. This time an American general named Benedict Arnold was the hero of the day. Riding horseback, he led three charges against the British lines. On one charge, British troops under young General Simon Fraser held their own.

"Pick off that Fraser!" Arnold shouted. "Get him and the day is won!" A moment later a sharpshooter aimed his rifle and fired. Fraser fell from his horse, badly wounded. His troops fell back. Soon Arnold also fell from his horse with a bullet wound in his leg. He was carried from the field.

But the Americans won the day. Burgoyne's bleeding, starving army dragged away toward Saratoga. Soon his army was completely surrounded. On October 17, Burgoyne surrendered his army of more than 5,000 British and Hessian troops.

The victory was the most important the Americans had won so far. It took some time for the news of this great victory to reach Europe. But when it did arrive it brought France, Britain's old enemy, into the war on America's side. Now America would have a powerful ally in its struggle for independence.

Chapter 12

BATTLE AGAINST WINTER

There was no food. Soap was as scarce as meat. Men's hands and feet were covered with sores. Bright new uniforms of a year before had turned into dirty rags. Men stood in the snow in bare feet.

This was Valley Forge, Pennsylvania, in the winter of 1777–78. It was the camp of General George Washington and his army. Only 20 miles away in Philadelphia, the British army was warm and comfortable. Each month more and more of Washington's men were dying of hunger, disease, and the cold. Sometimes the soldiers became angry. "We want meat! We want meat!" they would shout from their log huts. "No meat — no soldier!" they called out.

Finally the shouting died down. The starving men were too weak even to complain. All was quiet.

The Americans had won a great victory at Saratoga

only a few months before. France would soon send help. But in the meantime General Washington was desperate. He was busy sending letters. He wrote to Congress begging for clothing and for money to pay his men. He wrote to the governors of nearby states asking for food. Washington was angry. He knew that the states, like Congress, found it hard to raise money or supplies. Too many people thought it risky to lend anything to the government. After all, there was still a good chance that the war would be lost. But Washington was angry just the same. If only these people could see the suffering of his men, Washington thought, they would send help.

Help did come, though it was not what Washington expected. In February 1778, Baron Friedrich von Steuben arrived at Valley Forge. Von Steuben came from Prussia, a powerful German kingdom. He said he had been a general in the Prussian army. Actually Von Steuben had never been a general. He had never been more than a captain. But he was a fine soldier — and Washington's men needed training badly. Von Steuben was just the man for the job.

Von Steuben was a tough drill master. He drove Washington's men hard. He taught them how to use the bayonet. He taught them how to march with snap. He taught them how to move in formation. "Damn" was the first English word Von Steuben learned. He used it often. But Von Steuben was also a kind man. Washington's men respected him and worked hard for him.

Spring brought new hope to Valley Forge. Food, clothing, and rifles began to arrive. So did more men. France entered the war on America's side. In June, Washington's army marched away from Valley Forge. With the help of Von Steuben, it had been reborn. It had become a tough, well trained body of fighting men. The weaker soldiers had already deserted. Those who had stuck it out at Valley Forge were ready now for the hard fighting ahead.

Chapter 13

A MOST LOVED MAN

The teenage boy looked funny walking down the street in Philadelphia. His clothes were a mess. Extra socks and shirts stuck out of his pockets. He had a big loaf of bread under each arm. And he was chewing on a big roll. A young girl looked at him and burst out laughing. This funny-looking boy of 17 was young Benjamin Franklin. He had just run away from home in Boston. Some day he would become one of the greatest men in America. And the girl who laughed at him? She would become his wife.

Benjamin Franklin was born in Boston on January 17, 1706. He was the youngest son in a family of 17 children. Ben's father had a small shop where he made soap and candles. He was able to send Ben to school for only two years. Then Ben had to go to work, helping his father.

Ben didn't like making candles, and his father knew it. But Ben's older brother, James, had a printing shop. Would Ben like to become a printer? Ben liked to read. And there was a lot to read in a printing shop. So Ben said he would work for his brother.

At the age of 12, Ben started his new job. He became a very good printer. Then the two brothers began to have fights. Finally Ben ran away and settled in Philadelphia.

Ben was only 17, and "on his own." But he made a good living as a printer, and he also made a lot of friends. After a while he was able to open up his own printing shop. Ben worked hard. Soon he was printing his own newspaper. It sold more copies than any other paper in the American colonies.

In 1732 Ben began to print *Poor Richard's Almanac*. It had news of the weather, holidays, and the best time to plant seeds or pick grapes. But it also had many wise and funny sayings that Franklin made up. Some of them were:

"God helps them that help themselves."

"Little strokes fell great oaks."

"Lost time is never found again."

"Half the truth is often a great lie."

People loved Poor Richard's sayings. They bought many copies of the *Almanac*, and Ben became a rich man. He also became a leading citizen of Philadelphia. He did many things to make Philadelphia a good town to live in. He became its postmaster and speeded up the mail service. He started a fire department and a police department. He started its first library and first hospital. He also started the school that later became the University of Pennsylvania.

At the age of 42, Franklin had made enough money to quit business. He liked science and wanted to learn more about electricity. Franklin's most famous test of electricity was made in 1752. He flew a homemade kite in a thunder storm. At the end of the string he tied a key. Lightning hit the kite and went down the string to the key. Then an electric spark shot out from the key. This proved that lightning was electricity. Soon after, Franklin invented the lightning rod. This keeps houses from catching fire when lightning strikes them. Franklin won many honors for his work.

As time went on, Franklin became more and more active in public affairs. He had a gift for talking things over with people, and getting them to see that there was more than one way of looking at a problem. Long before the Revolutionary War broke out, Franklin went to England to defend the rights of the American colonies. First he was sent to represent the people of Pennsylvania. Later he represented Georgia and Massachusetts as well. Finally he became the spokesman in Britain for all 13 colonies. For many years he was quite successful at explaining the colonists' point of view on many government matters.

But later there were more and more outbreaks of violence in the colonies. There were riots against British taxes. British property was destroyed by mobs in some cities, especially Boston. Then Franklin's job became much harder. Sometimes the British leaders listened to him. Sometimes they did not. Finally Franklin felt he could not help the colonies any more in England. He sailed for home in March 1775.

When he arrived in Philadelphia, the Revolutionary War had already begun. Franklin was made the postmaster-general of the American colonies. Later he helped Thomas Jefferson write the Declaration of Independence.

Franklin was now 70 years old. But the American Congress had a big job for him. The Americans were not doing very well in the war against the British. They needed help. So Congress sent Franklin to France to ask for aid. The royal court of France fell in love with wise, old Ben Franklin. Crowds of people ran after him in the streets of Paris. There were pictures of him everywhere — on rings, watches, dishes, and vases. The French secretly sent supplies and money to the Americans. Finally, after the American victory at Saratoga, France openly joined the colonists in the war against the British. France sent ships and thousands of soldiers and guns to America. These men and ships and supplies helped to win the war for the Americans.

Franklin was a great hero in America after the war. He had a wonderful old age. He helped draw up the new U.S. Constitution in 1787, when he was more than 80. He was also elected head of the first anti-slavery group in the United States. His last public act was to ask Congress to end slavery.

Franklin died on April 17, 1790, at the age of 84. About 20,000 people in Philadelphia — almost half the city — went to his funeral. In France many people cried. Franklin was one of the most loved men in the world.

Chapter 14

HAYM SALOMON

Haym Salomon heard the loud knocking on the door.
He knew what it meant. British soldiers had come to
arrest him. Haym sent his young wife, Rachel, out of
the room. Then he opened the door.

"You are Haym Salomon, the Jew?" a British soldier asked.

"I am Haym Salomon. What is the charge?" he
answered.

"Treason against the King!"

Then Salomon was marched off to jail.

Haym Salomon was not surprised by his arrest. A
Polish Jew, he had come to New York before the
Revolutionary War. In Poland — and other countries
of Europe — Jews were forced to live in ghettos.
These ghettos were walled-off parts of cities. They
were like prisons. No one was allowed to enter or
leave the ghettos after dark. Many laws kept the
Jews poor. They had no rights as citizens. Some countries did not even let them practice their religion.

In America, Salomon and other Jews found freedom of religion and a chance to get ahead. Salomon went into business in New York and did well. By this time — 1772 — some Americans were already thinking of throwing off British rule. A group called the Sons of Liberty was ready to fight for American independence. Salomon loved freedom and soon joined the Sons.

When the American Revolution began, he became a secret agent. He helped wounded American soldiers and prisoners escape from the British. Sometimes he hid them in his house. He was arrested by the British in 1776, but later he was freed. Now, in August 1778, he was arrested again. This time, Salomon knew, he would be hanged.

Salomon was given a "trial" by four British officers. He was found guilty of treason and sentenced to hang the next morning. Death was only hours away.

The soldier who guarded Salomon's cell was a young German from Hesse. The British had hired many Hessians to fight for them against the Americans. Salomon spoke German well. He told the guard of an offer that the American commander, George Washington, had made. Washington said he would give land to any Hessian soldier who quit the British.

The guard liked the idea. He and Salomon made a deal. Salomon gave him a note to take to an American agent. The agent would then help the guard reach the American army. In return, the guard opened the lock on Salomon's door.

Running at night, hiding by day, Salomon reached the American army. Salomon was shocked by what he saw at the American army camp. The soldiers were dressed in rags. Almost all of them were hungry. They weren't even getting paid. They had no money to send home to their families. No wonder so many of them quit! Congress had no money to give the army. Why? It had no power to tax the states. It could only *ask* the states for money. And the states themselves found it very difficult to raise money.

Salomon had become sick in the British prisons. He would be no good to the Americans as a soldier. But — maybe he could help them with money. If only he hadn't left everything in New York. He couldn't go back there now. The British would get him. But what about Philadelphia? Philadelphia was in American hands. He could set up his business there.

Salomon made the long trip to Philadelphia, walking most of the way. When he got there, friends helped him get started again. Salomon was a very good businessman. Before long he was rich.

Salomon tried to see Robert Morris, the man who was in charge of raising money for Congress. Morris was a busy man. He had no time to see Salomon. But months later, Salomon got a letter from Morris. The letter said that General Washington needed $20,000 right away to keep the army going. Could Salomon get the money? Salomon dug into his own pockets for some of it. The rest he got from friends. Morris gave Salomon an IOU for the money. Salomon wanted no interest for the loan, but Morris said he must take one per cent.

After that, Morris asked Salomon for more and more money. Salomon worked day and night to get the money for him. Not many men wanted to lend money to Congress. They thought it was too risky. But Salomon never let Morris down. He handed over to Morris hundreds of thousands of dollars.

After the war, Salomon was "broke." He and his family now owed money to others. And Congress could not pay back to Salomon any of the money he had loaned it. Congress was still much too poor. It did not matter to Salomon. His reward was that he had helped America win its freedom.

Salomon tried to make money in business again. But by now his sickness had gotten much worse. He had worn himself out during the war. He died in 1785, at the age of 45, without a penny.

Chapter 15

LIBERTY'S PENMAN

The American captain rode hard through the hills and forests of Virginia. His horse was tired, but it was a race against time. British soldiers were on their way to Monticello, the home of Thomas Jefferson. They wanted to arrest the man who had written the Declaration of Independence. The American captain knew some shortcuts. He got to Monticello just before dawn, ahead of the British. He warned Jefferson to escape quickly. It was June 4, 1781. The Revolutionary War was not yet over.

Jefferson did not panic. He ate breakfast calmly. Then he sent his wife and children away to a safe place. Afterward he burned some important papers. Then Jefferson went outside to look through his telescope. He could see about 250 British soldiers riding fast toward Monticello. Jefferson mounted his horse and made his getaway.

Minutes later, the British soldiers rode up to the house. One of them pointed a gun at the head of one of Jefferson's black servants. "Tell me which way your master is gone," he said, "or I fire."

"Fire away," the servant dared the soldier. But the soldier did not fire. It wouldn't have done any good. Jefferson had escaped.

Thomas Jefferson was a man the British wanted to hang. He was born on a farm in Virginia on April 13, 1743. His father was a strong, tough pioneer who had chopped down woods to build his farm. His mother came from a rich family. Tom had a good life as a boy. He went swimming, fished, and hunted in the forest. He also learned to play the violin.

Tom went to college at Williamsburg, Virginia, when he was 16. At first he seemed more interested in fun than books. He went to horse races, saw plays, danced a lot, and played his violin. But later he studied hard, sometimes for 15 hours a day.

After college Jefferson became a lawyer. In one case, Jefferson tried to win freedom for a slave. Jefferson told the judge that "under the law of nature all men are born free." Everyone, he said, "comes into the world with a right to liberty."

Jefferson lost the case, but he never stopped fighting against slavery. Later on he helped put an end to the slave trade in Virginia. He also made a plan for a new group of states west of the Appalachian Mountains. His plan kept slavery out of these states. Jefferson also wrote against slavery in the Declaration of Independence. But some members of the Continental Congress did not agree with what Jefferson had written. All of his words about slavery were scratched out of the Declaration before it was voted on.

Jefferson himself owned slaves all his life, and he freed only five of them when he died. Jefferson treated his slaves with great kindness. Yet he believed that black people, even if freed, could never become really equal with whites. Jefferson's ideas about black people went along with those of most of the whites of his time. Yet Jefferson thought that slavery was bad for everyone, for whites as well as blacks. He felt that there could be no room for slavery in a democracy.

During the Revolutionary War, Jefferson became the "penman of liberty." Jefferson wrote in the Declaration of Independence that "all men are created equal." He said that all men have certain rights which cannot be taken away. Among these rights were "life, liberty, and the pursuit of happiness." These were daring ideas in a time when most people were ruled by kings and princes. Even today Jefferson's words are still used by people fighting for freedom. And when people say "all men are created equal," they mean *all* men — not just all white men.

One of Jefferson's ideas has caused many arguments down through the years. In Jefferson's day, the United States was mainly a country of small farms. It had few large cities. Jefferson hoped it would always stay that way. He did not like cities, and he did not want factories and industries in America. Farming was the best way of life for people in a democracy — farmers were "the chosen people of God," Jefferson said. They would be the backbone of freedom and liberty in America.

Jefferson was a man of ideas. His thought has had a great influence on America in many ways. He was also a man of action.

After the Revolutionary War, Jefferson became Secretary of State, then Vice-President, and finally President. He was also a farmer, an inventor, a scientist, and a designer of buildings. In his old age, he started the University of Virginia.

Jefferson died on July 4, 1826 — exactly 50 years after the Declaration of Independence was signed.

Chapter 16

SURRENDER AT YORKTOWN

The British drummer boy hammered at his drum as hard as he could. But the noise of the cannons drowned out his message. Gunsmoke curled around his legs. Finally the Americans and the French let up on their firing for a moment and the drum beat could be heard. The message was clear: the British were asking for a meeting.

A British officer stepped out waving a white cloth. Soon he was blindfolded and taken to General Washington's headquarters. The British officer had a message for Washington. Lord Cornwallis, the British commander at Yorktown, wanted to surrender. It was a great victory for the Americans and the French. It would end the Revolutionary War.

How was the victory won? In 1781 the British decided to try to knock Virginia out of the war. They built up an army of 7,200 men in Virginia. Lord Cornwallis took charge of this army and camped it at Yorktown, on the coast. Facing it was a much smaller army made up of Frenchmen and Americans.

General Washington had a much larger American army outside New York City at this time. And Washington had a big decision to make. Should he attack the British in New York? Or should he march south and strike against Cornwallis in Virginia? Washington favored attacking New York. If it were captured, the war might be ended.

Washington had a meeting with Count Rochambeau, the French commander. Rochambeau had an army of 5,000 men, but he was against an attack on New York. "The British are too strong in New York," he said. "It would be much better to attack Cornwallis in Virginia."

Washington and Rochambeau knew that their armies alone could not defeat Cornwallis in Virginia. They would have to have sea power as well. What if the armies trapped Cornwallis at Yorktown, and then Cornwallis sailed away on British ships? Cornwallis would have to be blocked on sea as well as land.

Washington and Rochambeau sent a message to French Admiral de Grasse in the West Indies. They asked for the help of his fleet. It was the middle of August before they got their answer. De Grasse was sailing for Yorktown to block a British escape by sea. He would also land extra troops.

Washington and Rochambeau began racing south to Yorktown with their troops. By the middle of September they had joined the small French and American army that was already there. And in the meantime, De Grasse had won a victory at sea. He had beaten a British fleet sent from New York to help Cornwallis. Now Cornwallis was hemmed in by land at Yorktown — and blocked at sea by the ships of Admiral de Grasse.

The Americans and their French allies had 16,000 men at Yorktown. Cornwallis had less than half that many. Soon the allied cannons were pounding the British defenses day and night. Then, on October 14, French and American troops attacked. They struck swiftly after dark. They captured two British outposts.

Allied cannons pushed closer to the front. Soon 100 of them were blasting the British lines. Now the British position was hopeless. Their defenses were smashed. Finally, on October 17, the British drummer boy began hammering out his message. Cornwallis was finished.

The victory at Yorktown was the end of the war. The British people were tired of this long and costly struggle. The peace treaty wasn't signed until April 1783. But Yorktown was the last big battle.

The Americans had won their War for Independence.

PART 3

A
MORE
PERFECT
UNION

WE THE PEOPLE

During the war years the 13 states had been under heavy pressure to live up to their name — the *United* States. The states had to cooperate with each other in order to win the war. But even then many of the states did not cooperate as much as they could have. There were times when Washington and his men wondered if the states had forgotten them. The national government was always short of money because the states did not provide enough.

Now that the war was over, the United States faced some hard tests. Would it be able to run its own affairs? Could it go on acting as a united nation? Or would it turn into just a loose union of 13 separate states?

For a time it looked as if the new nation might fall apart. It was run by Congress according to a plan called the Articles of Confederation. This *con*federal plan of government was nothing like the federal form of government we have today. The Articles gave Congress, which was the national government, very little power. It didn't even have the power to tax people.

As a result, Congress was too broke to keep up a strong army and navy. And it could not win the respect of other nations. Congress was also without power to control trade between states.

Lack of money was the new nation's biggest problem. Congress had come out of the war with large debts. So had the states. At first the Congress and the states tried to pay off these debts by printing paper money. But this didn't work, because the paper had nothing to back it up. Soon it became worthless. Later the states tried to raise money by increasing taxes. Many states raised their taxes on land, buildings, and the sale of food.

These taxes were especially hard on farmers. Riots and protests broke out among farmers in several parts of New England. In 1786 a large group of Massachusetts farmers joined an uprising. They were led by Daniel Shays, a Revolutionary War hero. Many of these farmers had been thrown off their land when they could not pay their debts and taxes. Some had been jailed for owing money. Shays and his followers took up arms against the tax collectors. They even attacked a courthouse of the state supreme court and drove a judge away at gunpoint. These men were angry, and they meant business.

Shays' Rebellion showed that many people were very unhappy with the way things were going in America. The British had been gone for only three years, and already the new nation faced an uprising. It showed that the government was too weak to keep order, too. Shays and his rebels had to be put down by *state* troops. The Articles of Confederation gave Congress no power to help the states preserve law and order.

Many American leaders were deeply worried about the new nation. Among them were George Washington, Alexander Hamilton, and James Madison. They wanted to change the Articles of Confederation to make the government stronger.

With this aim, the states agreed to hold a meeting in Philadelphia in 1787. But the men who met there decided that they would not be able to just patch up the Articles here and there. They decided to draw up plans for a new government instead. What they came out with was the U.S. Constitution. This Constitution has been the law of the land ever since.

Under the Articles of Confederation, Congress had no money to support an army. If trouble came up, states had to rely on their own part-time soldiers (above). Often these men did not look or fight much like soldiers. Below, an example of money printed by states.

Chapter 17

THE LEADERS GATHER

It was a sunny springtime Sunday in Philadelphia in 1787. The air was warm and fresh with the smell of budding leaves. Crowds of people lined the streets. Church bells were ringing and flags were flying. Revolutionary War veterans fired their muskets in welcome. Cannons boomed a salute. It seemed as if the whole city had turned out to greet this man.

Who was arriving? It was George Washington, America's hero and commander-in-chief during the Revolutionary War. Washington was wearing his old buff-and-blue uniform with three gold stars on each shoulder. He also wore a powdered wig under his three-cornered hat. Sitting straight and easy on his carriage seat, Washington didn't smile much. But his eyes looked very blue under their bushy brows.

"Speech, General! Speech!" shouted the crowds again and again. But Washington didn't stop his carriage to give a speech. He and the other men arriving in Philadelphia had far more important business to attend to.

America had run into serious trouble under the Articles of Confederation. Congress didn't have enough money to run the government. It had no way of making the states carry out its decisions. The states were jealous of their powers. In some ways they acted as if they were 13 separate countries. Many of the states went right on printing their own money, even after it was known to be worthless. Many of them charged their own taxes on goods coming in from foreign countries. Some even charged taxes on goods coming in from other states. Things like this would be hard on a country even in normal times. But right after a war, when the nation had debts to pay, they were even worse.

But it was Shays' Rebellion that upset American leaders more than anything else. It took a big force of state troops to put down these rebel farmers. And the governor of Massachusetts had to ask private businessmen to foot the bill for the troops. Neither the state nor Congress had the money.

Shays' Rebellion raised a question that frightened many people. What if other rebels took up arms? Would the states be able to put them down? What would happen if rebels took over a state government? What if several rebellions broke out? The whole nation, just getting started after a hard-fought battle for freedom, could fall apart.

It was clear to American leaders that the central government needed more power. The Articles of Confederation just didn't work. They would have to be done over from top to bottom.

Two leaders, James Madison of Virginia and Alexander Hamilton of New York, felt that it would be dangerous to wait too long. They sent out a call to all the states for a meeting, or convention, to do the job. It was to be held in Philadelphia, starting in May 1787.

Travel was slow in those days. It took a long time for some of the states' delegates, or representatives, to arrive. New Hamphire's men came late. Rhode Island never sent any at all. After long days of waiting, the delegates settled down to business. There were 55 of them in all.

What kind of men were these early leaders of the United States? They were mostly men of wealth and education. They were lawyers, businessmen, bankers, professors, and planters. About half of them were college graduates. This was unusual in a time when very few people went to college.

The men who met in Philadelphia were chosen by their states. Two of the most famous leaders were George Washington and Benjamin Franklin. Others were James Madison of Virginia and Alexander Hamilton of New York. But not all of America's great leaders helped write the Constitution in Philadelphia. John Adams was in England at the time. Thomas Jefferson, who wrote the Declaration of Independence, was in France. Patrick Henry, the Virginia patriot, would not go to the meeting. He was sure that it would come up with a Constitution that would take too much power away from the states.

Many of the delegates knew from the start that the old Articles of Confederation would have to go. There was no point in trying to patch them up. The real job of the delegates was to draw up a new plan of government — a new Constitution.

The first thing the delegates did was elect George Washington to head the meeting. They all agreed on this. But for a long time afterward they agreed on little else. Writing the Constitution was not an easy thing to do. No one knew it at the time, but it would take the delegates almost four months to finish their work.

Chapter 18

ONE SUMMER IN PHILADELPHIA

That summer of 1787 was a hot one in Philadelphia. But the men who sat in the State House kept all the windows and doors closed. They also posted guards at the doors. Why? Because they wanted the meeting to be free from all outside pressures. And they wanted their discussions to be secret. In fact, they didn't even have a secretary to take down the minutes of the meeting. These delegates wanted to be known for *what* they did, not *how* they did it.

Still, rumors of what was taking place in the State House did leak out. And today we know quite a bit about what went on there. One of the things that went on — and on and on — was argument.

Delegates of the large states argued with the delegates of the small states right off. One thing they argued about was how the new Congress should be set up. Under the Articles of Confederation, each state had one vote in Congress. But the delegates from the larger states now said: "We have more people and pay more taxes than the smaller states. So it is only fair that we should have more say in making laws." Delegates from the smaller states said: "We don't want to give up any of our rights and powers in the new Congress."

For a while it looked as if the two sides would never agree. But finally they worked out a *compromise* — a middle way that satisfied both sides. Instead of having just one house, the new Congress would have *two* houses. In the House of Representatives, the number of members from each state would depend on how many people it had. But in the Senate, each state, large or small, would have the same num-

87

ber of members — two. This way the House of Representatives would represent the people directly. The Senate would represent them through their states.

Another thing the delegates argued about was how much power the new government should have. Leaders of the large states wanted a strong national government. They wanted it to have much more power than the state governments. Delegates from the smaller states wanted a government that would be a fairly loose union of states. They wanted the states to keep much of the power they had under the Articles.

Again there was a compromise. The Congress was given many new powers. Now it would be able to collect taxes directly from the people. It could borrow money to pay the government's bills. It could control all business done with foreign countries as well as business between states. No state would be able to print and coin its own money any more. Now Congress would do that — and for the whole country. It would also be up to Congress, not the states, to run the mail service. Only Congress would be able to declare war and order men to serve in the armed forces.

All powers not given to the central government were left to the states. It was still up to each state to control all the local governments inside its borders. Cities, towns, and school districts would be under the states. Each state still had the power to regulate any business firm that operated only inside the state's borders. In fact, the state government was left in charge of almost everything that took place inside the state. The national government was in charge of affairs that went on between the states, or between the United States and foreign countries.

That was the way the new Constitution divided up the job of government between the United States and the separate states. It worked in 1789, the year the Constitution went into effect. It was tested by a bloody Civil War for four years, from 1861 to 1865. It is still working today.

Chapter 19

CHECKS AND BALANCES

The delegates in Philadelphia divided the job of governing America between the United States and the separate states. They also divided Congress into two parts — the House of Representatives and the Senate. But that was not the only dividing they did. They also divided the national government. They split it into three parts.

This was not an original idea. The delegates had borrowed it from a French thinker named Montesquieu. Montesquieu had written a famous book called *The Spirit of Laws*. In it he talked about the different kinds of government men had lived under. He showed that the worst kind of government is tyranny. Tyranny results when all the powers of government are held by one man, or one group of men. The best kind of government, Montesquieu thought, is one that is divided into three separate parts. When the government is divided into three parts, each part holds only *some* of the government's powers. Then each part, with its powers, can *check and balance* the other parts. The result of checks and balances, Montesquieu wrote, is freedom.

This made sense to the delegates in Philadelphia. So they divided the United States government into three parts, or branches. These branches are: the Congress, the Presidency, and the Supreme Court.

Congress was set up as the *legislative* branch of the government. It makes new laws.

The Presidency was set up as the *executive* branch. The President, or Chief Executive, carries out the laws of Congress and is the head of the government.

The Supreme Court was set up as the *judicial* branch. The Supreme Court settles arguments about the Constitution and hears the most important law cases in the land.

"Checks and balances" prevent any one branch of the government from becoming too powerful. They make each branch depend in some ways on the other two.

For example, the President has some control over the Supreme Court. He is the one who appoints a new member of the Court whenever an old one dies or retires. The Supreme Court has some control over the President, too. It can declare that a law strongly favored by the President is "unconstitutional" — not allowed by the Constitution. Congress often passes a law that it knows the President wants, or that he thinks is very important. But if the Court decides that the law goes against the Constitution, that law is tossed out.

The President and Congress check and balance each other also. The President can tell Congress what new laws he would like it to pass. He can call special sessions, or meetings, of Congress. Calling a special session of Congress shows that the President really wants it to pass laws that he thinks are badly needed.

The President can *veto*, or stop, any bill passed by Congress. If the President vetoes a bill, it does not become law in most cases. But Congress can check and balance the President by *re*passing the bill — passing it over his veto. It takes two thirds of the votes in Congress to do this, so it doesn't happen very often. Congress can refuse to give the President the money he needs to carry out his programs. The Senate can block any treaty the President makes with a foreign country. The President may ask a man to represent the U.S. in a foreign country, or to be a member of the Supreme Court. But if the Senate does not like the man, it can block the appointment.

If Congress thinks that the President himself is unfit for office, it can put him on trial. The House of Representatives can *impeach* the President, or charge him with crimes or bad conduct. Then the Senate can put the President on trial. Only once did Congress ever impeach a President and put him on trial. That was in 1868, and the President was Andrew Johnson. But the Senate could not collect enough votes against Johnson to remove him from office.

The Supreme Court and Congress check and balance each other in several ways. Congress can pass a bill. The President can sign the bill and make it a law. But someone may think that this law goes against the Constitution. He might get the Supreme Court to listen to his case. If the Supreme Court agrees with him — out goes the law. Sometimes this happens many years after a law has gone into effect.

Congress can remove a Supreme Court justice who does something Congress feels is wrong. Congress can also change the number of justices on the Supreme Court. Today there are nine justices. The first Court had only six. Congress can also make changes in the lower courts that feed cases up to the Supreme Court.

So Congress, the President, and the Supreme Court check and balance and control each other. Each one holds some of the government's power. None of them holds all of the power. Today, after more than 180 years, the checks and balances system is still working.

Chapter 20

THE BILL OF RIGHTS

It was the middle of September. A touch of autumn was in the air. Delegates were standing around in groups, shaking hands and saying good-by. Then, one by one and two by two, they climbed into carriages and rode out of Philadelphia. Their job, writing the U.S. Constitution, was done.

But there was still more work ahead before the Constitution could become the law of the land. The next step was to send it to the states to be *ratified* — that is, to be approved and accepted. Nine out of the 13 states had to ratify the Constitution before it could go into effect.

Already the new plan was running into trouble with some state leaders. Many of these leaders liked what the Constitution *said*. It was what it did *not* say that got them upset.

These leaders saw how the three-branch government would work. They saw how the states would still have many rights and powers under the national government. But they asked, What about the rights of the people themselves? How do we know that the people will keep their rights and freedoms? Where does the Constitution *say* that the people's rights and freedoms will never be taken away?

Nowhere in the Constitution did it say that a judge could not sentence a man to prison unless the man was proved guilty. Nowhere did it say that a man's

Bill of Rights

Congress of the United States,

begun and held at the City of New York, on Wednesday, the fourth of March, one thousand seven hundred and eighty nine.

The Conventions of a number of the States having, at the time of their adopting the Constitution, expressed a desire, in order to prevent misconstruction or abuse of its powers, that further declaratory and restrictive clauses should be added: And as extending the ground of public confidence in the Government, will best insure the beneficent ends of its institution:

Resolved, by the SENATE and HOUSE of REPRESENTATIVES of the UNITED STATES of AMERICA in Congress assembled, two thirds of both Houses concurring, That the following Articles be proposed to the Legislatures of the several States, as Amendments to the Constitution of the United States; all, or any of which articles, when ratified by three fourths of the said Legislatures, to be valid to all intents and purposes, as part of the said Constitution, viz.

Articles in addition to, and Amendment of the Constitution of the United States of America, proposed by Congress, and ratified by the Legislatures of the several States, pursuant to the fifth Article of the Original Constitution.

Article the first ...... After the first enumeration required by the first Article of the Constitution, there shall be one Representative for every thirty thousand, until the number shall amount to one hundred, after which, the proportion shall be so regulated by Congress, that there shall be not less than one hundred Representatives, nor less than one Representative for every forty thousand persons, until the number of Representatives shall amount to two hundred, after which, the proportion shall be so regulated by Congress, that there shall not be less than two hundred Representatives, nor more than one Representative for every fifty thousand persons. [Not Ratified]

Article the second .... No law, varying the compensation for the services of the Senators and Representatives, shall take effect, until an election of Representatives shall have intervened. [Not Ratified]

Article the third .... Congress shall make no law respecting an establishment of religion, or prohibiting the free exercise thereof; or abridging the freedom of speech, or of the press; or the right of the people peaceably to assemble, and to petition the Government for a redress of grievances.

Article the fourth .... A well regulated Militia, being necessary to the security of a free State, the right of the people to keep and bear Arms, shall not be infringed.

Article the fifth ...... No Soldier shall, in time of peace, be quartered in any house, without the consent of the owner, nor in time of war, but in a manner to be prescribed by law.

Article the sixth ...... The right of the people to be secure in their persons, houses, papers, and effects, against unreasonable searches and seizures, shall not be violated, and no Warrants shall issue but upon probable cause, supported by oath or affirmation, and particularly describing the place to be searched, and the persons or things to be seized.

Article the seventh ... No person shall be held to answer for a capital, or otherwise infamous crime, unless on a presentment or indictment of a grand jury, except in cases arising in the land or Naval forces, or in the Militia, when in actual service in time of War or public danger; nor shall any person be subject for the same offence to be twice put in jeopardy of life or limb; nor shall be compelled in any criminal case, to be a witness against himself, nor be deprived of life, liberty, or property, without due process of law; nor shall private property be taken for public use without just compensation.

Article the eighth ..... In all criminal prosecutions, the accused shall enjoy the right to a speedy and public trial by an impartial jury of the State and district wherein the crime shall have been committed, which district shall have been previously ascertained by law, and to be informed of the nature and cause of the accusation; to be confronted with the witnesses against him; to have compulsory process for obtaining witnesses in his favor, and to have the assistance of counsel for his defence.

Article the ninth ...... In suits at common law, where the value in controversy shall exceed twenty dollars, the right of trial by jury shall be preserved, and no fact, tried by a jury, shall be otherwise re-examined in any Court of the United States, than according to the rules of the common law.

Article the tenth ...... Excessive bail shall not be required, nor excessive fines imposed, nor cruel and unusual punishments inflicted.

Article the eleventh .. The enumeration in the Constitution, of certain rights, shall not be construed to deny or disparage others retained by the people.

Article the twelfth ... The powers not delegated to the United States by the Constitution, nor prohibited by it to the States, are reserved to the States respectively, or to the people.

ATTEST,

Frederick Augustus Muhlenberg, Speaker of the House of Representatives.

John Adams, Vice-President of the United States, and President of the Senate.

John Beckley, Clerk of the House of Representatives.

Sam. A. Otis Secretary of the Senate.

house could not be searched without a legal permit. And nowhere did it have a list of man's basic rights and freedoms.

The writers of the Constutition had *talked* about these things at their meetings. But they had not put such a Bill of Rights into the Constitution. Why? Because they knew that each state constitution already had its own bill of rights. The rights of the people, they thought, were already well protected.

The missing Bill of Rights almost wrecked the Constitution's chances of being adopted. Patrick Henry of Virginia was one of the people speaking loudest against it.

Most people said they liked the Constitution, Bill of Rights or not. But in some states, the "no" votes ran almost even with the "yes" votes. Still, by the end of a year, 11 states had voted to ratify. On March 4, 1789, Congress said that the new U.S. Constitution was in effect.

What was the first thing Congress did under the new government plan? It passed 10 amendments, or changes, to the Constitution. These first 10 amendments are the Bill of Rights that so many people had wanted.

Some of these first 10 amendments do not seem to be as important today as they once were. Take the Third Amendment, for example. The Third Amendment says that soldiers cannot be put up in a private home without the owner's consent — except in wartime. Hardly anyone pays much attention to this amendment anymore. But other amendments in the Bill of Rights seem to be just as important now as they were in 1789. Here are the ones that mean most to us today:

The First Amendment says that Congress cannot make laws to work for or against any religion. It says that Congress cannot make laws against freedom of speech or freedom of the press. It also says that Congress cannot make laws against the people's right to hold peaceful meetings — and to ask the government to correct wrongs.

The Fourth Amendment says that a person's house and belongings cannot be searched without a legal permit — a *warrant* — from a court.

The Fifth Amendment says that if a person is found "not guilty" in a trial, he cannot be tried again for the same crime. Nor can a person be forced to be a witness against himself — that is, he cannot be made to tell things about himself that would get him in trouble with the law. No person can be punished without "due process of law."

The Sixth Amendment says that a person accused of a crime must have a "speedy and public" trial by jury. The accused person must be told what he is accused of. Any witness who has something to say about the accused person must say it to the person's face. And if the accused person wants a lawyer but has no money for one, he may have a lawyer at government expense.

The Eighth Amendment says that an accused person does not have to put up "excessive bail." Bail is money left with the court when an accused person is released until his trial comes up. If a person is found guilty of a crime, his punishment must not be "cruel or unusual." If he has to pay a fine, it must not be too high.

The Bill of Rights was quickly ratified by the states. Then these first 10 amendments became a part of the Constitution. They are one of the main reasons why the Constitution has lasted so long.

Today the Constitution has 25 amendments. In a way, these show how well the Constitution was written in the first place. Why? Because *in* the Constitution it says that the Constitution can be changed, or amended, whenever change is needed. Yet only 15 amendments have been adopted since the original Bill of Rights 180 years ago.

In some ways the Constitution in 1789 was not as

democratic as it could have been — not by today's standards. The President and Senators were not to be chosen directly by the people. Instead, Senators were to be chosen by the state legislatures. And the President was to be elected by *electors* who were chosen by the state legislatures. But amendments changed this later on. Today Senators are elected directly by the people. Electors of the President are also chosen directly by the voters.

The Constitution did not outlaw slavery in the United States, either. The *word* slavery was never used in the Constitution. But the Constitution accepted slavery. If it had not done so, about half of the states would never have ratified it. It would never have become the new plan of government the nation needed so badly. Still, many of the delegates in Philadelphia hated slavery.

In many ways, the Constitution was the best and most democratic plan of government *for that time.* Most other countries were then ruled by kings or noblemen. Slavery was accepted in many countries also.

The men who wrote the U.S. Constitution in 1787 showed they were very wise. They knew that the Constitution was not perfect. Even Ben Franklin said that he did not agree with everything in it. But Franklin said he would sign it anyway, and hoped that the other delegates would do the same. Why? Because Franklin doubted that any other meeting would be able to make a *better* Constitution.

Other leading delegates backed Franklin's argument. One said that he would sign the Constitution "with all its faults." In the end, many delegates signed the document partly because they knew it could later be amended wherever it was necessary.

Today the U.S. Constitution is the oldest written national constitution in the world. Many new nations and governments still use it as a model when they write *their* constitutions.

PART 4

THE
NATION
EXPANDS

PUSH TO THE WEST

The United States was a large country at the end of the Revolutionary War. In fact, the new nation controlled an area more than twice the size of the original 13 colonies before the war. The peace treaty in 1783 gave the United States all of Britain's land from Canada down to Florida, and from the Appalachian Mountains to the Mississippi River.

Many of Europe's leaders were surprised by the peace treaty. They hadn't expected Britain to give up so much land. American leaders were pleased. In those days it was a long way from the Atlantic to the Mississippi. It looked as if the young republic had all the growing room it would need for a long time to come.

But then, in 1803, the United States signed another treaty — one that has been called "the greatest real estate bargain in history." By this treaty, the United States bought from France a huge piece of land called the Louisiana Purchase. The Louisiana Purchase was much larger than the area Britain had given up. It stretched from the Mississippi River to the Rocky Mountains, and from the Gulf of Mexico to Canada. This was about 828,000 square miles of some of the world's most fertile land. At a price of 15 million dollars, the United States paid three cents an acre for it.

Few Americans knew much about this new land they had bought. The government wasn't even sure where some of the borders were. Soon the U.S. was arguing with Britain about the border with Canada.

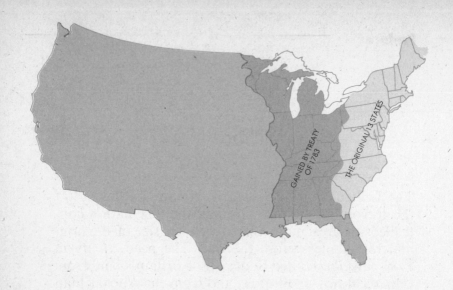

GAINED BY TREATY OF 1783

THE ORIGINAL 13 STATES

The U.S. argued with Spain about the border with Florida and Mexico.

These arguments were still going on when war with Britain broke out. Americans called it the War of 1812, or the Second War for Independence. Actually it was part of a bigger war that had started in Europe, between Britain and France. For several years the United States tried to stay out of the struggle. But finally, in 1812, the United States declared war on Britain.

The United States had two main reasons for going to war again with Britain. For one thing, the British navy had been seizing American ships that were trading with France. Sometimes American sailors were dragged from their ships and forced to serve in the British navy. This was called *impressment*.

A second reason had nothing to do with shipping. American settlers along the Great Lakes border with Canada were having a lot of trouble with the Indians. Most of the settlers felt sure that Britain was stirring up this trouble. Actually the settlers were causing their own trouble by taking over more and more Indian land. But after a big battle with the Indians in 1811, the Americans found some British weapons in an Indian village. This made the settlers angry. They demanded war with Britain. They wanted the U.S. government to march troops into Canada and take it over.

Southerners, too, wanted to take over more land. What they wanted was Spanish Florida. Spain was an ally of Britain's. So why not seize Florida? Southerners asked.

The War of 1812 did not go very well for the Americans. Their invasion of Canada failed. The British navy placed ships around U.S. seaports to shut off their trade. A British army marched into Washington, D.C., and burned down much of the city. American General Andrew Jackson did win a victory over the British at New Orleans. But by that time, 1815, the U.S. and Britain had already signed a peace treaty. Neither side gained or lost any land as a result of this treaty.

But after the war was over, the United States began to expand again. In 1818 the U.S. and Britain worked out a new boundary between Canada and the Louisiana Purchase. This agreement gave the U.S. a large piece of land that the two countries had argued about for years.

The following year, in 1819, the U.S. gained Spanish Florida. The U.S. had already taken over parts of it in 1810 and 1812. Then Andrew Jackson marched in with troops and took over the rest. The Spanish were too weak to stop the Americans, so they signed a treaty. By this treaty, Spain gave up Florida in return for five million dollars. The United States and Spain also drew a new boundary line between the Louisiana Purchase and Mexico, and all the way across America to the Pacific.

The ink was hardly dry on this treaty when Americans began moving over the new boundary into Texas. Texas was then Mexican territory, and the Mexicans welcomed new settlers. Mexico had just won its inde-

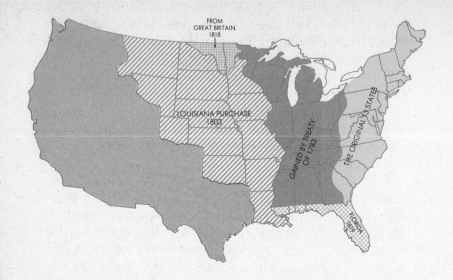

FROM
GREAT BRITAIN
1818

LOUISIANA PURCHASE
1803

GAINED BY TREATY OF 1783

THE ORIGINAL 13 STATES

FLORIDA 1819

pendence from Spain, and the country was very weak. Many Mexicans thought that American settlers would help to build up the country. But it turned out the American settlers did not like Mexican rule. Before long, they rose up in revolt and declared Texas independent. This was in 1836. The Mexicans were shocked and bitter.

Then, in 1845, Texas gave up its independence and joined the United States. This made the Mexicans boiling mad. At the same time, the U.S. government was putting pressure on Mexico to sell all the land between Texas and the Pacific. Mexico refused. Many Americans hoped that war would break out between the U.S. and Mexico. In 1846 it did.

The Mexican War lasted two years. American armies invaded Mexico and won battle after battle. Even Mexico City was captured. Finally Mexico asked for peace. In 1848 it signed a treaty that turned over to the U.S. all of California and most of what is today the American Southwest. This vast piece of territory was called the Mexican Cession. Five years later, the U.S. paid Mexico for a smaller piece of land called the Gadsden Purchase.

While the Mexican War was being fought, the U.S. and Britain came to a peaceful agreement on one more border. This was in the Pacific Northwest, between Canada and the Oregon Country. The boundary here was fixed where it is today, along the northern border of the state of Washington. Neither side was very happy with this border. But they agreed it was better than going to war again.

Between the peace treaty with Britain in 1783 and the Gadsden Purchase in 1853, 70 years had passed. Seventy years is a short time in the history of a nation. Yet during this short time the United States had grown by leaps and bounds. It had expanded from ocean to ocean, and from Canada to the Rio Grande. It had grown in area from a large nation into a giant nation — one of the largest in the world.

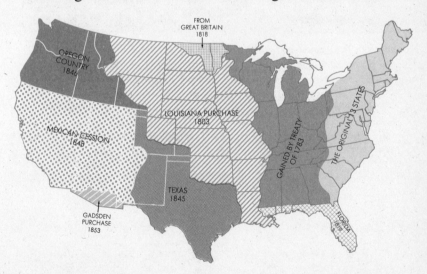

Many people said it was America's *Manifest Destiny* — its natural future — to expand the way it did. It certainly looks as if this was true. The United States grew through both war and peace. Some lands it bought. Some lands it got through talks and treaties with other countries. Other lands it conquered. It took Indian lands mostly by force.

Expanding on land and sea. Above, launching of the *Fulton the First*, the first steam-powered warship, in New York Harbor in 1814. Robert Fulton, the inventor, was an American. Below, first houses of the settlement that became known as Chicago, about 1820. Right, Daniel Boone, the pioneer who led thousands of settlers over the Appalachians into Kentucky and points West.

Tecumseh (left), a Shawnee chief, tried hard to unite Indian nations against the advance of the American frontier. He and his British allies were defeated in battle (above) in Canada during the War of 1812. Indians were not the only ones who took scalps in battle (upper right, an American soldier). Defeats and false treaties led to removal of many tribes to areas farther west (lower right, Sioux Indians).

Americans shooting bears (above) along the Mississippi River were "taming" the frontier. Many people today wish that wildlife had not been killed off on such a big scale. Below, a newspaper ad seeking settlers for Minnesota in 1858, the year territory became a state.

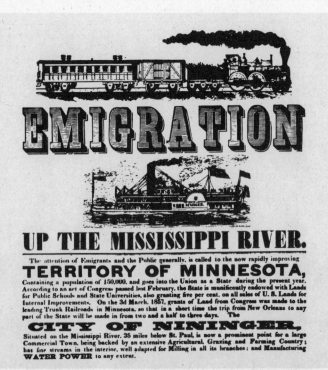

EMIGRATION

UP THE MISSISSIPPI RIVER.

The attention of Emigrants and the Public generally, is called to the now rapidly improving

TERRITORY OF MINNESOTA,

Containing a population of 150,000, and goes into the Union as a State during the present year. According to an act of Congress passed last February, the State is munificently endowed with Lands for Public Schools and State Universities, also granting five per cent. on all sales of U. S. Lands for Internal Improvements. On the 3d March, 1857, grants of Land from Congress was made to the leading Trunk Railroads in Minnesota, so that in a short time the trip from New Orleans to any part of the State will be made in from two and a half to three days. The

CITY OF NININGER,

Situated on the Mississippi River, 35 miles below St. Paul, is now a prominent point for a large Commercial Town, being backed by an extensive Agricultural, Grazing and Farming Country; has fine streams in the interior, well adapted for Milling in all its branches; and Manufacturing **WATER POWER** to any extent.

Bustling post office in San Francisco (above) in 1849, only a year after California became a part of the United States as a result of the Mexican-American War. Below, a homestead in the forests of Washington Territory.

Chapter 21

ALL THE WAY TO THE PACIFIC

Captain Meriwether Lewis froze in his tracks. Only 20 yards away — coming right for him — was a huge grizzly bear. Lewis was in a tight spot. He had just killed a buffalo — and forgotten to reload his rifle. Now there was no time. When the bear broke into a run, Lewis made a dash for a stream. He waded out into deep water. Then he turned, faced the bear, and held out his bayonet. The bear looked at Lewis in the water — and then suddenly ran away. So Lewis lived to tell the tale.

Grizzly bears, rattlesnakes, buffalo — these were some of the dangers Lewis faced every day. Why was he doing it? In those days, around 1800, the land west of the Mississippi River was mostly unknown. No one had really explored it. A few fur trappers had come back with stories of Indians, big prairies, and endless herds of buffalo. But there were few maps. No one was sure where its mountains, rivers, and forests were.

Then, in 1803, the United States bought a huge slice of this land from France. It was called the Louisiana Purchase. It went from New Orleans on the Gulf of Mexico up to somewhere in Canada, and from the Mississippi River on the east to the Rocky Mountains in the west. Many Americans were very eager to know what this new land looked like.

President Thomas Jefferson decided to send some men out to explore this territory — and to go beyond it, all the way to the Pacific Ocean. The man he chose for the job was his own private secretary, Captain Meriwether Lewis. Lewis was a strong, hardy Virginian. He had served in a number of army posts along the western frontier. He had also fought in several battles with the Indians. For a helper and friend to go with him, Lewis chose a fellow army officer, Lieutenant William Clark. Clark was a brave man with a lot of energy. He had also lived on the frontier.

Lewis and Clark carefully chose men and supplies for the trip. From St. Louis they would travel up the Missouri River in three boats. Then they would cross the Rocky Mountains on horses. Once across, they would paddle canoes down the Columbia River to the Pacific Ocean.

On May 14, 1804, the explorers and their men started out from St. Louis. The Indians they met were friendly — all except the Sioux. They gave the white men trouble. Once a group of Sioux surrounded Clark. They drew their arrows and took aim at him. But Lewis and 12 of his men aimed their rifles at the Indians. Finally the Indians let Clark go.

In November the explorers reached a large Indian village in what is now North Dakota. The explorers and the Indians got along well together. Lewis and Clark decided to spend the winter there.

Here they hired a French-Canadian trapper to help them with Indian languages. His wife, Sacajawea (Bird Woman), was a member of the Shoshone tribe that lived near the Rockies. Lewis and Clark would need horses from the Shoshones to cross the mountains. So they invited Sacajawea to join them.

In the spring the explorers started westward again. The trip up the Missouri River now became harder. Often the men had to tow the boats, standing in icy water up to their shoulders. After a long search, they found the Shoshones. With Sacajawea's help, they got horses for the trip across the Rockies.

The men suffered terribly crossing these mountains. The cold was bitter. Food gave out. Horses fell down the steep slopes. Finally the half-starved men reached the other side of the Rockies. There they set up camp among friendly Nez Percé Indians. They rested and got back their strength.

Then the men made dugout canoes for the trip down the Columbia River. Going over rough rapids was dangerous. Once the canoes were almost smashed. But, in November 1805, the explorers reached the Pacific. Clark wrote in his journal, "Ocean in view! Oh! the joy!"

Lewis and Clark had opened up the West. They had proved the continent could be crossed. They had made many maps and kept careful records of Indian tribes, plants, and animals. Traders and settlers would soon follow in their path. When Lewis and Clark got back to St. Louis in 1806, after a journey of 8,000 miles, they were national heroes.

Chapter 22

NEW PRIDE
FOR
THE NATION

"You must save yourself, Madam," cried the mayor
of Washington, D.C. "Half the city has already run
away. If the British win this battle, they will have no
mercy on Washington."

The mayor was standing at the door of the White
House. He was talking to Dolley Madison, the wife

of President James Madison. But Dolley Madison was not afraid. Instead, she tried to get the mayor to calm down. Then she went on helping to set the table for dinner.

This was August 24, 1814. The United States had been at war with Britain, in the War of 1812, for two years. During this time the British had not been able to do much fighting with the Americans. Britain was too busy fighting its old enemy, France, in Europe. But then, in 1814, the French suffered a great defeat. That left Britain free to send more of its forces against America. And now, in August 1814, the British meant business. They had landed an army in Maryland, and both Baltimore and Washington were in danger.

While Dolley Madison was getting ready for dinner in the White House, President Madison was only a few miles away in Bladensburg, Maryland. About 7,000 American troops were there, too. They were getting ready to fight a British army of about 4,000 men. This British army was made up of tough veterans of the wars against France. The American troops were mostly untrained militia.

The British brought rockets to the Battle of Bladensburg. These noisy, smoky weapons did little damage, but they scared the militia badly. Some of the Americans began running away from the battle. Soon the entire army was fleeing toward Washington.

There was only one bright spot for the Americans at Bladensburg. Joshua Barney, an old seaman who had fought in the Revolutionary War, was in command of some 500 sailors. There wasn't much need for sailors at Bladensburg, so Barney's brave seamen fought as soldiers instead. Most of them were free Negroes.

Before the battle started, President Madison asked Barney if his sailors would run from the British. "They don't know how to run," Barney answered. "They will die by their guns first."

Barney and his men held out against the British

114

for two hours. Finally Barney had to order his men to escape. He himself was taken prisoner with a bullet in his hip. The British liked Barney and treated him kindly.

While the Americans were fleeing Bladensburg, Dolley Madison was packing her husband's papers. Then a messenger brought her a note from Madison. It told her to leave Washington at once. Only then did she make her escape.

Soon the British entered the city. Some of their officers went into the White House. While they were there, they ate President Madison's dinner. Then they ordered their soldiers to make a big pile of the White House furniture, and set it on fire. Within a few minutes, the flames roared up the staircase and through the roof. The British also set fire to the Capitol and other government buildings. Smoke and flames rose high above the city. The light could be seen for miles.

After burning Washington, the British decided to attack Baltimore. On September 12, they landed their army about 15 miles from the city. While the army marched overland, the fleet sailed toward the city's harbor. Its aim was to knock out Fort McHenry, which guarded the city.

The next day, the British were surprised to find a large American army waiting for them outside Baltimore. This army was well armed and well trained. The British decided not to attack such a strong force until they had help from their fleet.

The British fleet was pounding away at Fort McHenry. It fired rockets and shells at the fort all day. On one of the British ships there was an American lawyer named Francis Scott Key. He had gone on board to ask the British to free an American prisoner. Key watched closely while the British tried to knock out the fort. Hour after hour went by, and darkness fell, but still the fort held out. At night, by the glare of the rockets, Key could see that the

American flag was still flying. Key felt so proud about the way the fort held out that he wrote a poem about it. Later this poem was set to music and became the American national anthem: "The Star-Spangled Banner."

After firing on Fort McHenry for a day and a night, the British decided they could not take Baltimore. The next morning they left.

The attacks on Washington and Fort McHenry gained nothing for the British. But the burning of their capital made many Americans very angry. And the brave defense of Baltimore filled them with pride. These feelings united them in the war against Britain for the first time since the struggle had started.

When the War of 1812 began, many Americans were against it. The people of New England especially hated the idea. They thought that the powerful British navy would blockade their seaports and ruin their trade. Actually, the British did not blockade New England until the last year of the war.

Some Americans felt that there was as much reason to fight France as Britain. France, too, had seized many American ships and forced sailors to serve its navy. But the British had given weapons to Indians on the frontier. This had made most Americans feel much angrier with Britain than with France. And besides, some Americans wanted to use the war as an excuse to add Canada and Florida to the U.S.

As it turned out, the United States did not win any land from Britain as a result of the war. Britain did not win any land from the United States, either. Peace came with the signing of a treaty in December 1814. Both sides were glad to sign this treaty. They were tired of the fighting.

The United States may not have "won" anything in the War of 1812. But it did gain a new spirit of patriotism — a feeling of pride as a nation. The American people had fought a Second War for Independence — and won their right to remain free.

Chapter 23

"OLD HICKORY"

No one had ever seen anything like it before. Woodsmen — rough men who lived in log cabins out West — were pouring into Washington, D.C. Many wore coonskin caps and muddy boots. Their mouths were full of chewing tobacco. These were real pioneers — farmers, hunters, and Indian fighters.

There weren't enough rooms for them in the hotels. So four or five of them slept together in a bed. Some slept on floors or on pool tables.

What were they all doing in Washington? They had come to see their hero, Andy Jackson, sworn in as President. Wasn't Andy "one of the boys"? Wasn't he born in a log cabin, just as they had been? Didn't his folks have to chop down trees to make a farm, just like theirs? Didn't Andy fight the Indians, just like they did? Andy wasn't one of those gentlemen fellows from the East, no sir.

No question about it — Andy was their boy. And now it was March 4, 1828, the day Andy was sworn in. Andy took the solemn oath and then rode on horseback to the White House. He was going to have a party there for important government men and their wives. The tables were all set up with good food and punch.

Andy's friends didn't want to go home. They wanted to see Andy in the White House. So they followed him to the White House and pushed their way in. Inside, some of them stood on fancy, velvet chairs to see their hero. Others pushed toward the food tables to eat. Plates were broken and food and drink were spilled on the beautiful carpets. Ladies in fine silk dresses fainted. Andy — President Jackson — was shoved against a wall. Friends kept him from being crushed by the crowd. Finally they helped him to escape. Andy spent his first night as President in a hotel.

Andrew Jackson — the hero of the "common man" — was born in the western part of the Carolinas in 1767. At that time it was wild, rough country, covered with forests of pine trees. The few houses, or cabins, were made of logs. Andy's father, a farmer, died a few days before Andy was born. He had hurt himself pushing a heavy log.

Andy wasn't a good student in school. He was too busy wrestling, racing, and jumping. But he did learn to read well. Few people in those parts could read or write. So Andy used to read the newspaper out loud to the farmers. One day, in 1776, he read to them about the Declaration of Independence. It had just been signed in Philadelphia.

When he was 13, Andy became a fighter in the Revolutionary War. Soon after, he was taken prisoner by the British. He was ordered to polish the shoes of a British officer. Andy had a hot temper and he refused to shine the officer's shoes. The officer hit Andy hard on the face with his sword. Andy had a scar there for the rest of his life.

After the war, Andy studied to become a lawyer. No one understood how Andy made it. He seemed to spend most of his time playing cards and making bets on horse races. But he did become a lawyer and then went to Nashville, Tennessee. This was the "Wild West" in those days. Andy's temper was always getting him into trouble. He fought a duel with one man and was hit by a bullet two inches from the heart. Then Andy fired his pistol and killed the other man.

Andy became a farmer and went into politics. He also became an Indian fighter. In the War of 1812, Andy led riflemen from Tennessee against the British and their Indian allies. He was so tough his men nicknamed him "Old Hickory." In 1814 Andy led his fighters into Florida and captured Pensacola. Then, in 1815, he led an American army against the British at New Orleans. This army was made up of Tennessee and Kentucky riflemen, Frenchmen, free Negroes, pirates from New Orleans, and some Indians. It was a sharp fighting force, and it won a complete victory over the British. At the end of the Battle of New Orleans, the British left behind 700 dead, including their commander. They also left about 1,400 wounded. Jackson's force lost only eight dead and 13 wounded.

The Americans and the British had already signed a peace treaty by this time. But the news from Europe had not arrived yet. If the news had reached America sooner, the Battle of New Orleans would not have taken place. As it turned out, Andy Jackson became a great hero in America because of the victory at New Orleans.

Three years later, in 1818, Andy led another army into Florida. At that time Florida was Spanish territory. But before long Andy and his men had captured almost all the Spanish towns and forts in the area. The following year, 1819, Spain signed a treaty and gave up all of Florida to the United States. Again Andy Jackson had made himself a hero, especially in the South.

Andy was elected President of the United States in 1828. He was supported by the common people everywhere. Rich people usually hated him. They thought he was too rough and didn't have the proper manners to sit in the White House.

Andy was a strong President. He fought hard against any group that seemed to be working for its own good ahead of the nation's good. He also fought hard against the idea that a state could disobey any U.S. government laws that it didn't like.

Above all, Jackson gave plain people the feeling that they had a voice in the government. He was especially popular with the farmers of the West and the factory workers of the East. To these people, Jackson was not only a voice but the living proof of a great idea. He stood for the idea that, in a democracy like the United States, even a man of humble birth and "low-class" background could rise to the top — and become President.

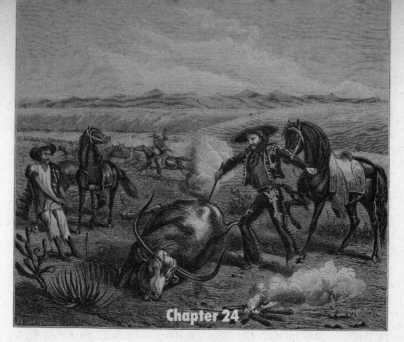

Chapter 24

THE VAQUEROS

The long, flat plains of New Mexico lie silent in the sunset. Somewhere far away a lone coyote wails into the evening shadows. For a long moment all seems empty and calm. Then, as the sun sinks down into the distance, the earth begins to tremble.

A low rumbling sound comes out of the west. Slowly it grows louder. A cloud of dust rises into the graying sky. The rumble becomes a roar. The earth seems to shake with excitement. Hoofbeats! The plain rocks with the pounding of hundreds of hoofs.

A herd of wild cattle thunders across the land. Their long horns are tossing. Their feet trample every living thing on the ground. Then, as they pass, the roar returns to a rumble. In a few minutes the plains are silent once more, and dark.

These dry plains rumbled often to the hoofbeats of great cattle herds. This was in the 1700's, when the first cowboys rode. These cowboys roped and branded the cattle while the animals were still wild. They rode the ranges of Texas and New Mexico long before any Americans moved into these lands.

Who were these first cowboys? They were Mexican Indians. They were the men who worked the ranches of Spanish missions. Many of the missions were both churches and forts, and they raised cattle on their lands to support themselves.

The Indians did not become cowboys by choice. In Mexico, their native land, they had been conquered by the Spanish. Then they were brought by force to what is now the American Southwest. Here, at the missions, they were taught by force how to ride and to rope. Many of the Indians had been branded on the cheek with the letter "G" — for *guerra*, the Spanish word for war. It is a fact that many of these first cowboys wore brands before their cattle did.

But these Mexicans became excellent cowboys. They took great pride in their work. And they took pride in the special outfits they wore. Around their heads they wrapped bright kerchiefs. They wore wide-brimmed hats to protect against sun and rain. Their knee-length pants buttoned on the sides and folded into buckskin shoes. Each man had a long knife fastened to his right leg. He also wore great slabs of cowhide, called *armas*. These covered his legs when he rode through thorns and heavy brush.

He called himself *vaquero* — the cowboy, or mounted herdsman. He carried no gun. His main weapon and tool was the *lariat*, a strong rawhide rope. Sometimes it was 110 feet long. With it he could bring a wild bull down to the ground — or a man, if necessary.

In the time of the vaquero, cattle were not herded to market. When it came time to take hides, the vaqueros held large-scale killings, called *matanzas*. They drove the cattle to the *matanza* grounds, roped them down with their lariats, and killed them with lances.

Their work was hard. So was their fun. A favorite sport was *corrida de toro*. Inside a fenced area, they let loose a lively bull. On horseback, the vaqueros waved capes at him. The bull charged. The vaqueros chased him. The aim? To grab hold of his tail, twist it, and dump the big bull to the ground.

The vaquero way of life came to an end in the 1800's. In 1821 Mexico threw off Spanish rule and became independent. Twelve years later, the Mexican government opened up the vast mission lands to settlers. Then the vaqueros were let go from the missions' control. They were free men.

But the vaqueros didn't have much time to know freedom. More and more American settlers began moving into the cattle lands. In 1836 they declared Texas independent of Mexico. Then, in 1846, the United States fought a two-year war with Mexico. When Mexico lost the war, it turned over to the Americans all of its land north of the Rio Grande River from Texas to the Pacific.

The Americans divided up the land into ranches of their own. Soon the vaquero had less room to ride. The land was no longer his.

Today great highways wind where cattle trails used to be. Large cities stand where many of the missions once ruled. The plains still roll out toward the horizon, flat and silent. But wild herds of cattle thunder across these lands no more. And the men who spent their lives following the herds under the hot western sun have vanished. They live now in our legends of the West — legends that live on in television and the movies.

Some five to seven million Spanish-speaking Americans live in the Southwest today. Many of them can trace their families back to the times when Mexico ruled this land. Some have proud vaquero blood. Most have come from Mexico more recently. All of these Americans look back with pride on the days when the vaqueros rode.

Chapter 25

ALAMO

"Within a very few days, we will all be dead. We must sell our lives as dearly as possible. For myself, I will fight as long as there is breath in my body."

These words were spoken by Colonel William B. Travis. Listening to him were 187 Texans. They were holed up in the Alamo, an old Spanish mission in San Antonio, Texas. Outside the walls, completely surrounding them, was a Mexican army of 5,000 men.

The leader of this army was the Mexican dictator Santa Anna. Not far away, from the top of the main church in San Antonio, a red flag was flying. The red flag meant "no quarter" — Santa Anna would take no prisoners. The date was March 5, 1836.

What had brought Santa Anna to the Alamo? He had come to put down a revolt. The Americans in

124

Texas had made trouble for the Mexican government for years. But now they had gone too far. They had already declared Texas independent of Mexico.

This was an outrage to the Mexicans. They had invited the Americans to settle in their country. They thought the American settlers would be thankful for the lands Mexico had given them. They thought the Americans would build up the country and become loyal Mexican citizens.

But most of the Americans who came were Protestants. Mexico had asked for Catholic settlers. Many of the Americans owned slaves. Mexico did not allow slavery. Some of the Americans were outlaws.

Before long, Mexico began passing laws that went against the settlers. One law said that no more slaves could come in. Another said that no more Americans could come in. Other laws began to take back some of the lands the settlers had been given. Then Santa Anna came to power in 1834. He did not trust any Americans. And the Americans did not trust him. Santa Anna sent troops into Texas to keep control of things. Soon after, the Americans revolted.

Santa Anna decided to teach the Americans a lesson. He marched into Texas with a large army. It reached San Antonio in February 1836. Most of the American rebels fled. But one small band withdrew to the Alamo. With these men were several friendly Mexicans. Some were women and children.

The Alamo was a strong fort, as well as a mission. Its walls were 10 feet high and three feet thick. It had about 20 cannons. Besides Colonel Travis, the Texans were led by Jim Bowie, inventor of the Bowie knife, and Davy Crockett, a famous scout.

For several days, Mexican cannons ripped the walls of the Alamo. Then, at five o'clock on the morning of March 6, a bugle call rang out. Thousands of Mexican soldiers began charging toward the Alamo's walls. The Texans grabbed their guns.

"Come on, boys, we'll give them hell!" Travis

shouted. Then the cannons of the Alamo blazed. One Mexican soldier saw 40 of his comrades fall dead or wounded around him. Others tumbled off ladders as they tried to climb the walls. Finally the Mexicans fell back. A second attack was also driven back by deadly fire.

Santa Anna's losses had been terrible. But he ordered a third charge. This time some Mexicans were able to get over the north wall. Then Colonel Travis slumped over a cannon, a bullet through his forehead. Other Mexicans climbed over the south wall and opened the gate. Mexicans poured into the Alamo.

Davy Crockett fought as long as he could stand. Finally he fell, riddled by bullets. The defenders who were left ran inside a building. There they made a last stand. All were finally killed.

In the Alamo's chapel, Jim Bowie lay sick on a cot. Women and children huddled around him. When the Mexicans rushed in, Bowie was waiting. He fired two pistols until he, too, was cut down by bullets and bayonets. Before long, all the defenders in the chapel were slain.

Santa Anna's victory had cost him 1,500 dead and wounded. But for Texans the Battle of the Alamo stood for the highest in bravery and heroism.

Later, at the Battle of San Jacinto, another Texas army met Santa Anna again. With shouts of "Remember the Alamo!" this army smashed the Mexican forces and captured Santa Anna himself. Then the prisoner signed a treaty giving Texas its freedom.

Texas was now an independent republic. But Santa Anna and the Mexican government could not accept this fact. Mexican maps still showed Texas as a part of Mexico.

The leaders of Texas wanted the United States to let Texas into the Union as a state. But Texas was kept waiting for a long time. Finally, on December 29, 1845, Texas entered the Union as the 28th state.

Chapter 26

THE BATTLE OF BUENA VISTA

A Mexican army of 15,000 men was marching north. Its aim: to destroy a much smaller American army at a mountain pass in Mexico. Its leader: Santa Anna, the man who had captured the Alamo.

It was February 1847. The United States and Mexico were at war. How did it come about?

In March 1845, the United States had invited the Republic of Texas to join the Union. Mexico had never accepted the loss of Texas. It warned that if Texas joined the United States, it would mean war. At the same time, the U.S. was putting pressure on Mexico to sell California. Mexico refused.

Then the U.S. sent an army into Texas under General Zachary Taylor. This army marched through Texas and up to the banks of the Rio Grande. The Rio Grande, Texans said, was their border with Mexico. But the Mexicans claimed the Rio Grande was well inside the border of Mexico. Soon Mexican and U.S. troops were fighting. Finally, on May 13, 1846, the United States declared war on Mexico.

The U.S. carried the war to the heart of Mexico. In February 1847, Santa Anna learned that Zachary Taylor was at Buena Vista (Beautiful View) with an army of less than 5,000 men. Most of them were untrained volunteers. Santa Anna saw his chance and decided to attack. Taylor, called "Old Rough and Ready" by his men, welcomed another fight. He placed his men in position in a mountain pass. There they would have an advantage over Santa Anna's forces.

On February 22 — Washington's birthday — Santa Anna attacked at Buena Vista. All that day, American riflemen and cannons beat back the Mexicans. As they fired, bands played "Hail, Columbia" and men shouted, "Honor to Washington!" When darkness came, the fighting stopped. Both armies shivered through a night of rain.

The next day, Santa Anna lined up his troops for an all-out attack. Mexican bands played sacred music. The Mexican soldiers and horsemen wore uniforms with bright colors. They were red, green, yellow, crimson, and blue. Some carried silk banners and long, handsome feathers. They shouted "Viva!" (long life!) to their leaders. They made a wonderful sight as they marched proudly to their positions. Some of the

American soldiers were a little scared of them.

Finally the battle was on. The Mexicans hit hard and fought bravely, but the Americans drove them back. Late in the afternoon, another Mexican force opened a powerful attack. Bullets could not stop it. Many Mexicans fell. But others swept forward, shouting "Viva! Viva!"

General Taylor calmly watched the fighting from the saddle of his horse. One bullet ripped through the front of his coat. Another tore his left sleeve. Near him cannons were firing. "Double your shot!" Taylor shouted to his men.

The cannons blasted the brave Mexicans at short range. Soon Santa Anna's men could stand the pounding no longer. They fell back into the mountains and the firing stopped. It was a close battle, but the Mexicans had lost twice as many men as the Americans.

On September 14, American troops under General Winfield Scott entered Mexico City. A few months later, Mexico signed a peace treaty with the United States. By this treaty, Mexico signed over to the U.S. a huge block of land called the Mexican Cession. It included all of what today are the states of California, Nevada, and Utah. It also included parts of Arizona, New Mexico, Colorado, and Wyoming. Mexico also agreed that the Rio Grande would be the boundary of Texas. In return for all this land, the United States paid Mexico 15 million dollars. The U.S. also agreed to pay all the money that Texas citizens said Mexico owed them.

Five years later the United States paid Mexico 10 million dollars for another piece of land. This was the Gadsden Purchase, named after the American agent who arranged the sale. The Gadsden Purchase was much smaller than the Mexican Cession. But it finally settled the boundary between the two countries. Today this land makes up the southern parts of Arizona and New Mexico.

PART 5

A
PEOPLE
APART

FROM SERVANTS TO SLAVES

The first Africans arrived in the English colonies in 1619. A Dutch ship sold the Africans as slaves at Jamestown, Virginia. There were 20 in all. Soon they were put to work in the tobacco fields.

The number of Africans in America grew slowly at first. In 1649 there were still no more than 300 in all of Virginia. Most of the work on the farms of the South was done by white servants. These servants were usually poor people who could not afford to pay their way from Europe to America. So they signed contracts, or agreements, with landowners in the New World. They agreed to work as servants for a set number of years. In return, the landowners paid the servants' way across the Atlantic. After a term of four to seven years, the servants were free. Then they might start farms of their own. When they got enough money together, they might have servants, too.

The first Africans who came to the English colonies were sold as slaves, but they were not *bought* as slaves. The English had never had slaves in England, so they didn't really know what slavery was. For the first 40 years or so, most of the Africans in America were thought of and treated as servants. Like the servants who came from Europe, they became free after a number of years.

Some blacks did well after freedom. In 1651 a black man named Anthony Johnson paid the Atlantic passage for five white servants. They helped him work his land for a time and then became free themselves.

But later the blacks lost their place as servants and became slaves. How did this happen? It started with the idea that not enough settlers were coming to the colonies to build them up. Colonial leaders were worried because word had gotten back to Europe that life in America was very hard. Many people did not want to settle in a new land where they would have to work as servants for a long time. So some of the colonial leaders began to cut down the number of years a newcomer would have to be a servant. They passed other laws, too, to make America more attractive to newcomers — to newcomers from Europe, that is.

But the leaders of the colonies did not need to change things to get Africans to come. The Africans were brought to America by force — shipload after shipload. So, instead of getting shorter, the black man's years of service got longer. Finally many whites came to think that black people could be kept on as servants — for life.

Another thing that worked against the blacks was the farming system that grew up in the South. Many farms in the South were becoming very large. They were called plantations. Plantations that grew crops such as tobacco or cotton could make big profits if they had cheap labor. Whose labor was cheapest? The black man's. The black man's labor was cheapest because his term of service was never "up."

Finally many white people said, "Why not make slaves of the blacks? That way we will always have the cheapest possible labor supply." So the white leaders began to pass laws that set black people apart from all other people who came to America.

The new laws said that black servants *belonged* to their masters — like property. Black people's *children* belonged to the masters, too. And all black servants could be bought and sold as their masters saw fit. It took many years for the colonies to pass all the laws that changed black people from servants into slaves. But by 1700 or so most of the work was done.

After 1700 black slaves were brought to America in large numbers. By the time of the Revolutionary War, half the people in Virginia were slaves. In South

132

Carolina there were twice as many blacks as whites.

For people from Europe the trip to America was usually very hard. But for the blacks from Africa it was a horror. First they were torn by force from their homes in Africa by cruel slave traders. Then they were jammed into ships. Usually they were squeezed into every inch of space below deck. Chained together, they were allowed on deck for fresh air only a few minutes each day. Their food was usually rotten and their water unfit to drink.

It took weeks for sail ships to cross the Atlantic. Many slaves died of sickness and bad food on the way. No one knows *how* many. Some killed themselves by jumping into the water. Some jumped overboard two at a time, still chained together. Those who tried to rebel were often shot or beaten to death.

In America the Africans were sold in slave markets. Families were often broken up, never to see each other again. What was ahead? For most it was a lifetime of hard work with no pay, poor food, and unhealthy living quarters. Many came to know the crack of the whip.

From 1700 to 1800 about seven million Africans were taken by force to various parts of the New World. About half a million were brought to America. Almost all of them went to the South. Slaves were not needed as much on the smaller farms of the North.

In 1808 the United States passed a law against bringing any more slaves into the country. But many slaves were still brought in against the law. By this time many white Southerners had come to believe that their "way of life" depended on slaves.

As time went by, slavery spread over more and more of the South. It spread into the Southwest as well. The problem of slavery would divide the nation very deeply in the years to come. In the end it would lead the nation into the worst war in its history — the Civil War.

Africans were captured in their homeland by slave traders. They were chained and sometimes branded like cattle (above) before they were crammed into ships. Those not chained often jumped overboard — but the artist who drew picture opposite forgot to show chains. In America, Africans were sold at auction to the highest bidder. In early colonial days, white servants (below, left) were also sold.

Many slaves led lives of misery in America. They never knew when their white owners might sell them. Families were often broken up. Above, a daughter says good-by to her parents — perhaps forever. Below, a black family on the auction block. Opposite, an auction house in Atlanta and a poster advertising a slave sale.

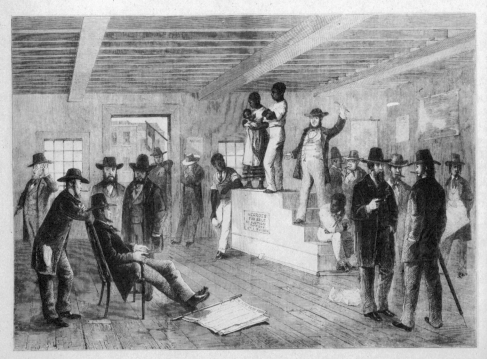

"Am I not a man and a brother?" This picture and plea appeared in an anti-slavery book published by abolitionists in the North. Abolitionists were strongly against the spread of slavery into the West, and wanted to abolish it in the South. They wrote hundreds of books, pamphlets, and articles about the evils of slavery.

135,000 SETS, 270,000 VOLUMES SOLD.

UNCLE TOM'S CABIN

FOR SALE HERE.

AN EDITION FOR THE MILLION, COMPLETE IN 1 Vol., PRICE 37 1-2 CENTS.
"   "   IN GERMAN, IN 1 Vol., PRICE 50 CENTS.
"   "   IN 2 Vols., CLOTH, 6 PLATES, PRICE $1.50.
SUPERB ILLUSTRATED EDITION, IN 1 Vol., WITH 153 ENGRAVINGS,
PRICES FROM $2.50 TO $5.00.

The Greatest Book of the Age.

The most famous of all abolitionist books was *Uncle Tom's Cabin,*
written by Harriet Beecher Stowe (above) in 1852. Abolitionists
were hated in the South and were often attacked in the North as
well. Below, a mob sets fire to an abolitionist printing house.

Some Northern whites had extreme feelings about blacks — both for and against. Above, a New York mob has hanged a black man. This happened during the Civil War, when many whites placed the blame for the war on black people. Below, abolitionists in Philadelphia welcome a black man who has mailed himself to freedom — in a box.

While some Northerners helped blacks escape and fight off slave-catchers (above), others went on attacking abolitionist presses.

While abolitionists in the North raised a louder and louder outcry against the evils of slavery, the lives of both slaves and masters in the South went on much as usual. Strict laws called "black codes" kept all blacks, the free ones as well as slaves, firmly "in their place" in the South. It was against the law to teach a slave how to read or write, so most slaves had no way of knowing much about the abolitionists or the "slavery question" that divided whites.

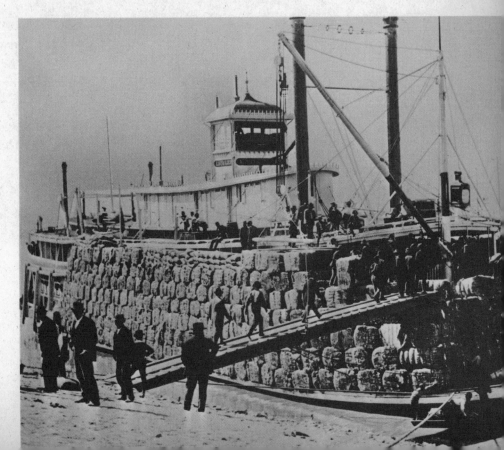

Chapter 27

NAT TURNER'S
REBELLION

It was the dead of night on the Travis plantation in Virginia. All was quiet. Masters and slaves were asleep. But six men armed with a hatchet, an ax, and some clubs were creeping toward the Travis house. These six men were slaves. They were about to start the biggest slave uprising in U.S. history.

Their plan was to march from one plantation to another, killing the slave-owners. They would also call on the slaves to join them in an attack on Jerusalem, the county capital. If they could capture the town, their revolt would become famous. Then maybe all the other slaves would revolt for miles around. If the attack on Jerusalem failed, they would retreat to a swamp. From there they would fight on. They would gather more followers and one day they would take over the whole state of Virginia.

The leader of this revolt was a slave named Nat Turner. As a boy, he had quickly taught himself to read and write. Once, when he was older, he had been whipped very hard. The whipping left Turner with scars for the rest of his life.

Turner was a religious man and prayed very often. He believed that he heard voices that were messages from God. They told him that one day he would do some great work. But Turner did not know what this would be.

Then one day Turner felt that he was seeing a vision. He believed that he saw black spirits fighting white spirits in the sky. He saw blood dripping from the heavens. Now Turner felt that he understood what he was to do. He was to lead the slaves in a battle for freedom.

Turner waited for a sign to begin his work. He waited nearly three years. On February 12, 1831, there was an eclipse of the sun. Turner took this to be his sign. He then told his plan to four slaves he felt he could trust. Together they set July 4 as the date for the revolt. But Turner let that day pass without doing anything.

Then, in August, Turner was sure he saw another sign. For three days the sun seemed to turn a greenish-blue color. For three nights there was "blood on the moon." Turner called a meeting of his trusted followers. It was held in a forest on August 21. There they were joined by another slave. The six men decided the revolt would start that night at the house of Joseph Travis, Turner's master. Travis had not been a hard master. But he was not going to escape.

After dark, the six men moved quietly toward the Travis house. Once inside, they killed the whole family. They took all the guns they could find. Then they went to other houses, murdering people in their beds. Only a few slaves joined the revolt. Most of the slaves were either too frightened or felt loyal to their masters. They would not take part in the uprising.

That night Turner's band killed 55 men, women, and children. The next morning it headed for Jerusalem. But soon the slaves ran into armed white men. After some firing, the slave band broke up. Turner went into hiding only two miles from the Travis home. Then Virginia state militia took a terrible revenge. Hundreds of innocent blacks were shot down in cold blood. Dozens of others were tortured to make them "talk."

Finally 53 slaves were put on trial. Some were hanged, some sent away, and a few let go.

Turner was caught in October and tried for murder. He pleaded "not guilty." His lawyer asked him if he had any regrets about what he had done. Turner said no. He went to his death calmly on November 11.

Nat Turner's uprising shook the whole South. Whites everywhere were very frightened. Hard laws were passed against all Negroes, free or slave. Many white Southerners went on saying that slavery was good for the Negro. But after Turner's uprising, that became much harder to believe.

Chapter 28

SHE RAN
A RAILROAD

A poster in a Southern railroad station read:
"WANTED — dead or alive — Harriet Tubman.
A reward of $40,000 is offered for capture."

Why was such a large reward offered for the capture of a black woman? Perhaps the answer is in the story of her life.

Harriet Tubman was born a slave on a Maryland plantation in 1821. She was whipped constantly while she was a child. Harriet had scars on her neck from these beatings. Once, when she was 14, she tried to save a slave from a whipping. She stood in the way of the "boss" with the whip. The slave started to run. Then the boss picked up a heavy iron weight. He threw it at the slave, but it struck Harriet's head instead. Harriet fell to the ground. For days she lay near death. Finally Harriet grew stronger. But she never got completely well. She had a deep scar where the iron weight had hit her. And, for the rest of her life, she had strange sleeping spells.

Harriet hated being a slave. She knew that one day she would escape to the North where there was no slavery. One night she and two of her brothers made a break for freedom. But the brothers soon became frightened and turned back. Harriet went on alone. She hid by day and moved north by night. She guided herself by the North Star. She was also helped by the "Underground Railroad." The railroad had no trains. But it had many "stations." These were the homes of people who hid slaves by day and sent them on to other homes after dark. This underground network stretched from the South to the North and to Canada. With its help, Harriet finally reached Philadelphia.

She was free at last. But Harriet was not content. She wanted to help her family and other slaves to escape. Soon she became a "conductor" on the Underground Railroad. She made trip after trip to the South to lead slaves to freedom. In all, she helped free more than 300 slaves. Among them were her aged parents and the rest of her family. Southern slave-owners tried again and again to capture her. Finally they offered the $40,000 reward.

Here is the story of one of her adventures:

Led by Harriet Tubman, 11 slaves walked through the woods. They were cold and hungry. It was so dark they couldn't see each other. Yet Harriet Tubman led them as if the sun were shining. The slaves spoke in whispers. They were frightened — they could hear the barking of dogs. They knew that slave-catchers — men who made money catching escaped slaves — were after them.

Harriet knew of a stream nearby. It was icy cold, but Harriet told the slaves to go into the water. She knew the dogs could not smell them in the water and track them down. The slaves stayed in the water until they no longer heard the dogs barking.

They walked for days and weeks — and still they were far from freedom. Their goal on this trip was Canada. Why Canada instead of one of the Northern states? Because in 1850 Congress passed a new law. This law said that any runaway slaves caught in the North would have to be sent back South. So after 1850 the Underground Railroad went to Canada.

The group went on together, hiding in swamps when danger was near. One day while they were hiding, Harriet began to wonder where the man from the next "station" was. He was very late. She prayed that the Underground Railroad had not let her down. Finally a man did come. He told Harriet he had a horse and wagon and food in his barn. That night Harriet went to the barn. There was everything the man had promised. "Praise God," the slaves said. They were another step closer to freedom.

Years later, while the Civil War was being fought, Harriet served in the Union Army. She served as a nurse, a scout, and a spy. Then when the war was over, she took several children and old poor people into her home.

Harriet Tubman died at the age of 93 in the town of Auburn, New York. For three days all the flags in Auburn were flown at half-staff in her honor.

SCHOOL FOR COLORED GIRLS

Chapter 29

GROWING CONFLICT

The North and the South were arguing again. But this time it seemed worse than ever before. One Southern Congressman said that the North had started a fire which only "seas of blood" could put out. Thomas Jefferson said that the argument alarmed him like "a fire bell in the night."

What was this argument about? Why were the North and the South so deeply divided?

The argument was about slavery. It was 1819, and the two sections of the nation were bitterly opposed on the question of letting a new state into the Union. The state? Missouri. The question? Whether or not slavery should be allowed in Missouri.

Many people in the North were against slavery. A few were so against slavery they wanted to abolish it — get rid of it altogether. Other people had a different view. "If we must have slavery," they said, "then let it be kept in the South. We don't want it here in the North." In the South, most white people felt that slavery was not wrong. About three out of four whites in the South owned no slaves at all. But even these Southerners, or most of them, felt that slavery was good for the South.

Southerners also felt that slavery should be allowed to spread. Not into the North, if the North didn't want it. But they saw no reason why it shouldn't spread into the new lands opening up to the west.

These differences between the North and the South came to a head in 1819. At that time the nation had 22 states. Eleven of them were slave states and 11 were "free" — that is, they were states where slavery was not allowed. Until 1819 there had been a fixed line between the slave states and the free states. It was this line that divided the nation into two sections, too — the North and the South. This line ran along the southern border of Pennsylvania and then west along the Ohio River to the Mississippi. The line stopped at the Mississippi — that was where the Louisiana Purchase began.

Part of the Louisiana Purchase had already been divided up into *territories* — blocks of settled land that were waiting to be let into the Union as states. And now, in 1819, the Missouri Territory was ready for statehood. But the big question was: Would Missouri join the Union as a free state or as a slave state? The people of Missouri had asked Congress to admit their territory as a slave state.

Many Northerners were very upset about this. For one thing, Missouri would make the 12th slave state in the Union while the free states were only 11. That meant the slave states, or the South, would have two more votes in the Senate than the free states, or the North. "And not only that," Northerners said. "Letting Missouri join the Union as a slave state might set an example for the whole Louisiana Purchase. What would happen if *all* the territories in the Louisiana Purchase came in as slave states? Then where would we be?"

Southerners shot back, "Missouri has a right to enter the Union as a slave state, if that is what its people want. The North has no right to stand in the way." Southerners were also angry about the matter of balance in the Senate. "The North has more people than the South. It has far more Representatives in Congress than we have. So if the South has two more Senators than the North, it will even things out a little."

The "Missouri Question" was argued far and wide. In Congress there were shouting matches about it. Some people thought the nation might split up over the issue. Jefferson called it a "fire bell" — a warning of danger to the country.

Luckily the Missouri Question was settled after a few months. The two sides reached a *compromise* — a peaceful settlement that both could accept. This happened in 1820. It was called the Missouri Compromise.

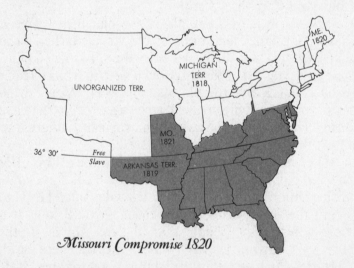

Missouri Compromise 1820

By this compromise, Missouri was let into the Union as a slave state. The northern part of Massachusetts was let into the Union as a new free state — Maine. That way the Senate balance between slave states and free states was kept — at 12 to 12. As for the rest of the Louisiana Purchase, a line was drawn through it. North of this line, except for Missouri, slavery was not allowed. South of it, slavery was legal.

Many people, North and South, gave a sigh of relief. Now the nation had a new line between its slave and free sections. It looked as if the slavery question had been settled.

And it *was* "settled" — for a while. But 30 years later, in 1850, it flared up again. This time the land in question was the Mexican Cession. California wanted to come into the Union as a free state. Southerners were against this because California would give the free states a 16 to 15 edge over the slave states in the Senate.

This big clash was also settled by a compromise. By the Compromise of 1850, California came into the Union as a free state. The rest of the Mexican Cession was left to decide the slavery question for itself. If the settlers who moved into it wanted slavery, they could have it. If they didn't want slavery, they could outlaw it.

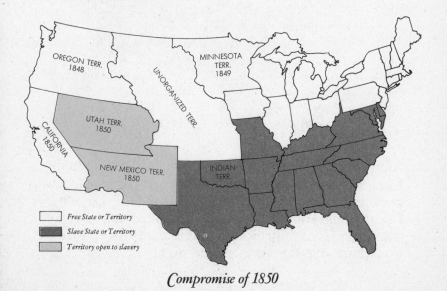

Compromise of 1850

Again the nation heaved a great sigh of relief. But this time the period of "good feeling" between the North and the South was very short.

A third and even more bitter clash over slavery came in 1854. This time Congress passed a law which did *not* settle the matter. Instead, the Kansas-Nebraska Act of 1854 undid the old Missouri Compromise. The new law said that the people of Kansas and Nebraska could decide for themselves whether or not they wanted slavery. This raised a storm of protest in the North. Why? The Kansas-Nebraska Act meant that the Louisiana Purchase no longer had a dividing line between its free and slave sections.

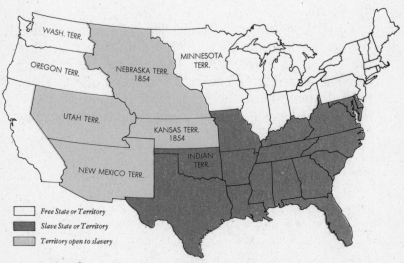

Kansas-Nebraska Act 1854

No one knew it at the time, but *all* the laws of Congress on the question of slavery in the territories were about to be thrown out. The U.S. Supreme Court would soon be hearing a very important slavery case. The Court's decision on this case would throw the whole question into a new light.

Chapter 30

THE DRED SCOTT CASE

Was a slave a human being with rights — or was he just a piece of property? If he was taken into a state or territory that did not allow slavery, did he become free — or was he still a slave? Could a slave become a citizen?

Questions like these divided the nation very deeply in the 1850's. By this time large numbers of people in the North had been won over to the movement against slavery. Many of them wanted to do away with slavery — *abolish* it — everywhere in the country. These people were called *abolitionists*.

In the South, most whites believed that they had a

right to own slaves. Not only that — they also believed they had a right to bring their slaves with them into any part of the country, even free states and territories. People who felt this way believed that the abolitionists were nothing but trouble-makers.

Finally, in 1857, it looked as if the whole question of slavery in the territories would be settled by the U.S. Supreme Court. This was because of a Missouri slave named Dred Scott. Years earlier Scott had been taken by his master from the slave state of Missouri to the free state of Illinois. Later he had been taken to the free territory of Minnesota. Then he had been brought back to Missouri.

In Missouri a group of abolitionists decided to help Dred Scott win his freedom. They backed him in a legal battle through the state courts. They argued that, because Scott had been taken to a free state and to a free territory, he must have become a free man. He was no longer a slave when his master brought him back to Missouri. This argument was heard in the courts of Missouri for 10 years. Finally it was taken to the U.S. Supreme Court.

On March 6, 1857, the Supreme Court was packed with people. They had come to hear the Court's decision on the Dred Scott case. Excitement was high. People who were for slavery and people who were against it both hoped the decision would be on their side. A hush fell over the crowd as Chief Justice Roger Taney led the other eight judges into the courtroom. Five of the judges, including Taney, were Southerners.

When the judges were seated, Taney began reading the decision. His words ran like electricity through the audience. Taney said:

1. The words "all men are created equal" were never meant to apply to Negroes. The men who founded the country and wrote the U.S. Constitution had believed that Negroes were "an inferior class of beings" — not as good as white people. Because of

that, Negroes had "no rights which the white man was bound to respect."

2. Negroes could not become citizens of the United States. In fact, Dred Scott did not even have the right to take his case to court.

3. Slave-owners had a right to take their slaves with them into any part of the nation, North or South. Why? Because slaves were only "articles of merchandise" — that is, property.

4. The Missouri Compromise, which said there could be no slavery north of Missouri, was illegal. In fact, any law of Congress that barred slavery from any place in the nation was illegal. Congress could not take away the Southerner's right to his slaves any more than it could take away the Northerner's right to his mule, his horse, or any other piece of property he owned.

Only two judges of the Court, both from the North, were against the decision of the other judges.

Many Southerners were joyful about the Court's decision. Slave-owners felt that they had won a great victory. But in the North and West, mass meetings of protest were held. More and more people felt drawn to the abolitionist movement. And more and more people were attracted to the Republican party — the party that was against the spread of slavery into the territories.

Some abolitionists were very discouraged by the Supreme Court's decision. But Frederick Douglass, one of the leading fighters against slavery, said: "My hopes were never brighter than now. . . . The Supreme Court is not the only power in this world. . . . Judge Taney cannot pluck the silvery star of liberty from our Northern sky."

Four years after the Dred Scott decision, Americans would be fighting each other in the Civil War. The long conflict between the North and the South over the slavery question would be one of the main causes of that war.

PART 6

DIFFERENT DRUMMERS

AN AGE OF REFORM

Can human beings ever hope to live in perfect fairness and harmony with each other? Can the nations they set up, and the ways of life they live, be changed for the better? During the first half of the 1800's, there were many people in the United States who said *yes* to these questions. These people, who wanted to make life better for everyone, were called reformers.

The main goal of some reformers was to help people who needed special care in some way. A doctor in Boston set up the first center in America for the care of blind people. In Hartford, Connecticut, another man opened a school for the deaf. Dorothea Dix, a New England schoolteacher, spent most of her life trying to improve conditions for the mentally ill.

Reformers such as Frederick Douglass and William Lloyd Garrison were leaders of the fight against slavery. Garrison used such strong words against slavery that many people called him a fanatic — a person who goes "too far." But neither Garrison nor Douglass would take back anything they said about the evils of slavery. These men had many enemies, but they also won large numbers of people to the anti-slavery cause.

Other reformers fought for different causes. A young lawyer named Horace Mann fought for the right of every American child to have an education at public expense. As a result of his work, free public schools were opened in many areas that had never had them before. Mann's ideas about education caught on even more after he died. Today there are free public schools throughout America and in many other countries as well.

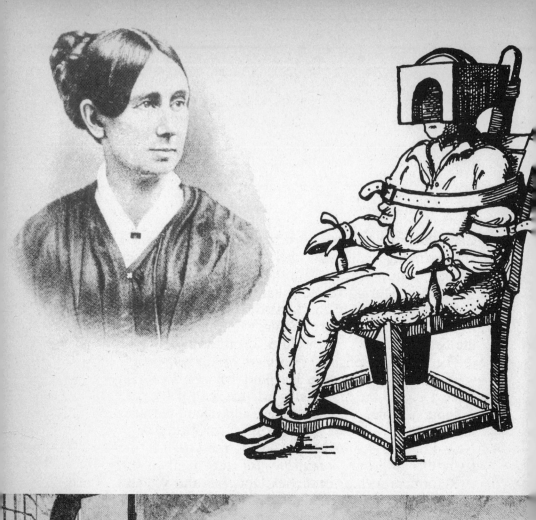

Reformers in America in the 1800's had plenty of problems to work on. Dorothea Dix (upper left, opposite page) spent years of her life trying to get better care for the mentally ill. Some of the conditions she was fighting are shown here: a patient strapped into a chair; another man strapped into a box (above) and turned around and around "to bring back reason"; a woman imprisoned in a tiny cage called "the crib" (below). Lower left picture shows an alcoholic — a "sinner"— being visited by his "sinful" children.

Some reformers fought for the idea that in a democracy every person must have a free education. Above, a costly private tutor teaching children at home; below, adults learn to read in a school "out West."

A horse-and-wagon "school bus" in Virginia in the late
1800's (above). Free public schools were common in most
areas of the U.S. by this time, but schools were often
a long way from where many of their students lived.
A teacher and her class, made up of students of all
ages, posed for the picture below in 1888, in Nebraska.
Early schools in the prairie country, like the houses
people lived in, were usually built of sod blocks.

Chapter 31

SHE CARED

She cared about the poor, the sick, and the insane. Especially the insane, or mentally sick. In her day, very few people did. There were no hospitals for the insane then. Mentally sick men, women, and children were put in jails or poorhouses. Conditions in these places were usually awful. The insane were often locked up in dark cages, closets, or cellars. Many were chained. They were often whipped by cruel or ignorant keepers. They had little or nothing to wear and got very little to eat. They sometimes looked like skeletons.

But this woman, almost alone, changed these conditions. Her name was Dorothea Dix. Because of her, new hospitals were built and the mentally ill began to get better treatment. Kindness began to take the place of chains and the whip. As a result, many mentally sick people got better.

Dorothea Dix was born in Maine in 1802. In those days, Maine was mostly woods. There were few people and few roads. Dorothea lived in a lonely log cabin. Her father was a traveling preacher. Usually he was paid with food. Sometimes he wasn't paid at all. Then Dorothea and her two brothers would go hungry.

Dorothea hated the lonely, dreary life she led. At 12, she ran away. She lived for a while with her grandparents in Boston. Later she went to live with some cousins nearby.

At 14, Dorothea became a schoolteacher. Before long, she was running *two* schools. One was for children who could pay. The other was for poor children. Dorothea worked very hard. She hardly had time to sleep. She got up at four o'clock in the morning to study and read her Bible. Sometimes she didn't go to sleep until midnight.

The strain was too much for her. Her health finally broke down. She spent years trying to get well. All the while, she wanted to help other people. But what could she, a woman, do? Women had few rights in those days. They couldn't even vote. Then one day in 1841 Dorothea was asked to visit a jail near Boston. Would she read the Bible to the women prisoners there? Dorothea went to the jail. She was shocked by the conditions she saw there. It was winter, but there was no heat to keep the women warm. Some of the prisoners were insane. Dorothea told the jail keeper to put in a stove to heat the place. The jail keeper told her "crazy people" didn't need stoves.

Dorothea became very angry. She felt she had to do something to help these people. For the next two years, she traveled all over Massachusetts. She went to every jail, poorhouse, and home where insane people were kept. She made notes about the terrible things she saw. She saw men and women chained in dark, filthy rooms behind iron doors. One man was even kept in a hole in the ground. Many of the insane were very thin from lack of food. Dorothea rubbed the hands of one man, trying to warm them. She spoke to him kindly and told him that some day he could go home. The man said nothing, but a tear ran down his cheek.

Dorothea then gave all her notes to an important man in Massachusetts. He read them to the state's lawmakers. Many people did not like what Dorothea had done. They felt that the insane were no better than wild animals. Others believed that the insane were being punished for their "sins." But finally the lawmakers voted money for a decent hospital for the mentally ill. Good treatment and kindness helped many of the patients get better.

Dorothea then traveled all over the United States visiting the insane. She traveled more than 60,000 miles. Nothing stopped Dorothea, not even her bad health. Everywhere she talked to lawmakers about "God's poor and outcast." She would not take "No" for an answer. In almost every state she visited, money was voted for new hospitals for the insane. Dorothea, who never married, called these hospitals her children.

Later Dorothea went to Europe to help the insane. In the Civil War, she became head nurse for the U.S. Army. After the war, she trained nurses to care for the mentally ill.

Dorothea Dix died at the age of 85 in 1887. A doctor said, "She was the most useful and amazing woman America has ever produced."

Chapter 32

FATHER OF FREE SCHOOLS

How would you like to go to a one-room school with a dirt floor? The windows are broken and the doors don't shut well enough to keep out the cold.

The roof leaks when it rains. There are no blackboards, charts, or maps on the walls. But there is a whip in the room. And every once in a while the teacher uses it — on "bad" students.

This is the way a lot of schools were in the early 1800's. About one school out of three was very run-down. Yet those who were students in them were *lucky*. In those days, most children did not get much schooling. Many of them lived on farms that were too far away from schools. Thousands of city children had to work in factories 10 to 12 hours a day.

A reformer named Horace Mann wanted to do something about this. Even as a boy he wanted to. When he grew up, he could have made a lot of money as a lawyer. But he took a school job at low pay instead.

Horace Mann was born in a small Massachusetts town in 1796. As a child he worked from morning to night on his father's farm. It was a hard life. He had little time to play, and he never went to school more than 10 weeks a year. But Horace liked books. He read every history book in the town library.

Horace thought he wanted to be a lawyer. Every chance he got he studied the subjects he needed to get into college. When he got to college, Horace was the best student in his class. He was also the most popular.

Horace Mann became a good lawyer. He was tall and thin and his eyes seemed to shine when he talked. In 1827 he was elected to the Massachusetts legislature. He worked hard to help the sick and the poor. But most of all he wanted to do something about the schools.

In 1837 a state Board of Education was set up to improve the schools in Massachusetts. Horace Mann was asked to become its head. The pay was very low. Many of Mann's friends told him not to take the job. "Stick to the law," they said. "Some day you'll be governor of the state." But Horace Mann took the job anyway. It meant that on most days he would have to skip lunch to save money.

Why did Mann give up being a lawyer to go into education? Because he believed that in the United States *everyone* had to be educated. In Europe only the ruling classes and the very rich got an education. The rest of the people didn't matter. But in the United States, Mann said, the *people* are the rulers. Democracy — rule by the people — cannot work unless everyone goes to school.

Mann traveled to almost every town and village in Massachusetts. Everywhere he went he told the people why they needed good schools. He got them to vote money for grade schools that were clean and well run. He got them to vote money for building high schools and for setting up libraries in the schools. Mann also set up special colleges to train better teachers.

Many people did not like the work Mann was doing. They said that schools for poor children were a waste of money. Why should they pay school taxes for children who didn't need an education? People who felt this way tried hard to stop Mann's work. But Horace Mann could not be stopped. In fact, many other states began to copy the work Mann was doing in Massachusetts. Countries in Europe began to copy it too. Horace Mann became known as the "father" of free public schools for all children.

Chapter 33

"I WILL BE HEARD"

An angry mob dragged William Lloyd Garrison through the streets of Boston. They put a rope around his neck. They wanted to hang him. But the mayor of Boston was able to stop the mob just in time. He put Garrison in jail for a while to protect him. It was October 21, 1835.

Why did the mob want to hang this man? Because he ran a newspaper that was very strongly against slavery. It was called *The Liberator*. Many Northerners at this time hoped that slavery would die away by itself. Or they thought that the government might be able to get rid of it slowly, step by step. But William Lloyd Garrison was not willing to wait. He wanted slavery ended *right away*. He fought against slavery day and night.

Slavery had never taken hold in the North the way it did in the South. And by this time all the Northern states had passed laws against slavery. But there were still many people in the North who did not like Garrison. They said he was a trouble-maker. If people in the South wanted slavery, they said, that was *their* business. Many workers in the North were afraid they would lose their jobs if the slaves were freed. The blacks, they said, would work for less money. And there were factory owners and other businessmen in the North who made their money from cotton. They did not want to see an end to slavery, either.

So Northern mobs often attacked people who were in the movement against slavery. The people who wanted to end slavery right away were called *abolitionists*. They were a favorite target of the mobs. Their lives were not safe. But Garrison — and other abolitionists — would not quit. Garrison was not afraid of anyone. Nothing could make him stop writing and talking against slavery. When he started his newspaper, Garrison said:

"I am in earnest. . . . I will not excuse [anyone]. I will not retreat a single inch. *And I will be heard!*"

Garrison made many enemies by taking a stand like this. But he also won many friends. And he lived to see the day when slavery was ended in the United States.

William Lloyd Garrison was born in a small town near Boston in 1805. His father was a drunk who left the family when William was three years old. Many times as a boy William had to beg for scraps of food. Many times he went hungry.

When he was nine, William had to leave school and go to work. After a while, he became a printer's helper on a newspaper. William liked good writers. He read their books at night. When he was only 17, he began to write articles for the newspaper.

Later William Garrison became the editor of a Baltimore newspaper that was against slavery. He could not understand the American people of his time. They were very proud of the Declaration of Independence which said, "All men are created equal." Yet they did not seem to care that millions of blacks were slaves. "I am ashamed of my country," Garrison said.

In 1831 Garrison started his own paper, *The Liberator*, in Boston. He didn't pull any punches when he wrote against slavery. He used very strong words. Many people — even some who were against slavery — did not like him for this. One minister said that Garrison did not write "like a Christian gentleman." Garrison did not care. "Men shall either like me or dislike me. There shall be no neutrals," he said.

Garrison also started one of the first groups to fight against slavery. It was called the American Anti-Slavery Society. Many people laughed at it at first. But by 1840 it had 250,000 members.

Once while he was in jail, Garrison wrote:

"Keep me as a prisoner, but bind me not as a slave. Punish me as a criminal, but hold me not as a chattel [slave]. Torture me as a man, but drive me not like a beast."

At home, Garrison was a kind husband and father. Most people were amazed when they met him for the first time. They thought he would be rough and tough, like his newspaper articles.

Garrison did not think that force was the way to end slavery. He was against war. He thought slavery should be ended by peaceful means. But when the Civil War broke out, Garrison gave his support to President Lincoln and the North.

In 1865 slavery was ended everywhere in the United States by the 13th Amendment. Garrison then stopped printing *The Liberator*. The battle he had fought for more than 30 years was won.

Chapter 34

FREEDOM FIGHTER

"I will run away. I will not stand it. I would rather be killed running than die as a slave."

It was Frederick Douglass talking. He was making a speech in Nantucket, Massachusetts, in August 1841. Douglass was telling his audience how he felt when he was a slave. The audience was shocked. This tall, handsome young man had once been a slave!

Yes, it was true. This man, who became one of the greatest leaders of the fight against slavery, was born a slave. The year was 1817. The place was a plantation in Maryland. While still a boy, Fred was sent to live with his master's relatives in Baltimore. The wife of his new master taught him to read and write. For Fred, nothing was more exciting. But then Fred's master stopped his lessons. He did not think it was good for a slave to know how to read and write. In fact, it was against the law to teach a slave to read or write. White Southerners did not want slaves to get any "dangerous ideas."

When his lessons were stopped, Fred knew for the first time how evil slavery really was. He dreamed of freedom from that day on.

When he was 16, Fred had his darkest hours as a slave. His master hired him out to a very cruel man named Edward Covey. Covey was known as a "slave-breaker," because he knew how to break the spirit of any slave who did not act like a slave. Covey whipped Fred without mercy many times. Finally Fred could take it no more. When Covey tried to whip him again, Fred put up his fists. He and Covey fought for nearly two hours. Finally Covey quit. He never tried to give Fred a whipping again. Fred was lucky. Some slaves who fought back were severely punished — or even killed.

Frederick Douglass was 21 when he decided to escape to New York. At the time, he was working in a Baltimore shipyard. He borrowed the papers of a free Negro sailor and dressed himself in a seaman's outfit. Then he got on the train for New York. It was a dangerous trip. Slave-catchers were always on the lookout for runaway blacks. But Douglass made it safely to New York. There he got in touch with people who belonged to the Underground Railroad. They sent him to New Bedford, Massachusetts.

Douglass wanted to live quietly. He did not want to do anything that would let slave-catchers know where he was. But then he was asked to speak at an anti-slavery meeting in Nantucket. Despite the danger, he accepted. Soon other anti-slavery meetings wanted him as a speaker.

Douglass was a fine speaker. Large crowds came

to hear him wherever he went. Sometimes they were not very friendly. In a few towns, Douglass was beaten by angry mobs. But he went on speaking just the same.

Douglass spoke so well that he ran into trouble. Some people began to doubt that he had ever been a slave. He sounded too well educated. Actually, Douglass had never gone to school. He was well educated because he had read a great number of books on his own. But the leader of one anti-slavery group told Douglass he must *prove* he was a runaway slave.

As a result, Douglass wrote a book about himself called *The Narrative of the Life of Frederick Douglass*. In it he told all about his life as a slave. He named his masters and he gave his own real name — Frederick Augustus Bailey. Soon slave-catchers were sent to arrest him. Douglass decided to go to England to escape them.

Douglass liked England, and many Englishmen liked him. They got together and bought his freedom from his ex-master. Then Douglass returned to the United States and started an anti-slavery newspaper. He called it *The North Star*, after the star that guided runaway slaves at night. When the Civil War broke out, Douglass became a friend and adviser to President Lincoln. He was one of the first people to advise Lincoln to let black soldiers serve in the Union Army. Lincoln thought it was a good idea, but other people in the government were against it. The war was two years old before any Negroes were allowed to be soldiers. And even then they had to serve in separate, all-black regiments. But Douglass' two sons were among the first to join up.

After the Civil War, Douglass held several different posts in the government. But it was his brave fight against slavery that people remembered best. In this battle, there was no greater hero than Frederick Douglass.

THE
DECLARATION
OF INDEPENDENCE

When in the Course of human events, it becomes necessary for one people to dissolve the political bands which have connected them with another, and to assume among the Powers of the earth the separate and equal station to which the Laws of Nature and of Nature's God entitle them, a decent respect to the opinions of mankind requires that they should declare the causes which impel them to the separation.

We hold these truths to be self-evident, that all men are created equal, that they are endowed by their Creator with certain unalienable Rights, that among these are Life, Liberty and the pursuit of Happiness. That to secure these rights, Governments are instituted among Men, deriving their just powers from the consent of the governed. That whenever any Form of Government becomes destructive of these ends, it is the Right of the People to alter or to abolish it, and to institute new Government, laying its foundation on such principles and organizing its powers in such form, as to them shall seem most likely to effect their Safety and Happiness. Prudence, indeed, will dictate that Governments long established should not be changed for light and transient causes; and accordingly all experience hath shown, that mankind are more disposed to suffer, while evils are sufferable, than to right themselves by abolishing the forms to which they are accustomed. But when a long train of abuses and usurpations, pursuing invariably the same Object evinces a design to reduce them under absolute Despotism, it is their right, it is their duty, to throw off such Government, and to provide new Guards for their future security. — Such has been the patient sufferance of these Colonies: and such is now the necessity which constrains them to alter their former Systems of Government. The history of the present King of Great Britain is a history of repeated injuries and usurpations, all having in direct object the establishment of an absolute Tyranny over these States. To prove this, let Facts be submitted to a candid world.

He has refused his Assent to Laws, the most wholesome and necessary for the public good.

He has forbidden his Governors to pass Laws of immediate and pressing importance, unless suspended in their operation till his Assent should be obtained: and when so suspended, he has utterly neglected to attend to them.

He has refused to pass other Laws for the accommodation of large districts of people, unless those people would relinquish the right of Representation in the Legislature, a right inestimable to them and formidable to tyrants only.

He has called together legislative bodies at places unusual, uncomfortable, and distant from the depository of their Public Records, for the sole purpose of fatiguing them into compliance with his measures.

He has dissolved Representative Houses repeatedly, for opposing with manly firmness his invasions on the rights of the people.

He has refused for a long time, after such dissolutions, to cause others to be elected: whereby the Legislative Powers, incapable of Annihilation, have returned to the People at large for their exercise: the State remaining in the mean time exposed to all the dangers of invasion from without, and convulsions within.

He has endeavoured to prevent the population of these States: for that purpose obstructing the Laws of Naturalization of Foreigners: refusing to pass others to encourage their migration hither, and raising the conditions of new Appropriations of Lands.

He has obstructed the Administration of Justice, by refusing his Assent to Laws for establishing Judiciary Powers.

He has made Judges dependent on his Will alone, for the tenure of their offices, and the amount and payment of their salaries.

He has erected a multitude of New Offices, and sent hither swarms of Officers to harass our People, and eat out their substance.

He has kept among us, in times of peace, Standing Armies without the Consent of our legislatures.

He has affected to render the Military independent of and superior to the Civil Power.

He has combined with others to subject us to a jurisdiction foreign to our constitution, and unacknowledged by our laws: giving his Assent to their acts of pretended legislation:

For quartering large bodies of armed troops among us:

For protecting them, by mock Trial, from Punishment for any Murders which they should commit on the Inhabitants of these States:

For cutting off our Trade with all parts of the world:

For imposing taxes on us without our Consent:

For depriving us in many cases, of the benefits of Trial by Jury:

For transporting us beyond Seas to be tried for pretended offences:

For abolishing the free System of English Laws in a neighbouring Province, establishing therein an Arbitrary government and enlarging its Boundaries so as to render it at once an example and fit instrument for introducing the same absolute rule into these Colonies:

For taking away our Charters, abolishing our most valuable Laws, and altering fundamentally the Forms of our Governments:

For suspending our own Legislatures, and declaring themselves invested with Power to legislate for us in all cases whatsoever.

He has abdicated Government here, by declaring us out of his Protection and waging War against us.

He has plundered our seas, ravaged our Coasts, burnt our towns, and destroyed the lives of our people.

He is at this time transporting large Armies of foreign Mercenaries to compleat the works of death, desolation and tyranny, already begun with circumstances of Cruelty & perfidy scarcely paralleled in the most barbarous ages, and totally unworthy the Head of a civilized nation.

He has constrained our fellow Citizens taken Captive on the high Seas to bear Arms against their Country, to become the executioners of their friends and Brethren, or to fall themselves by their Hands.

He has excited domestic insurrections amongst us, and has endeavoured to bring on the inhabitants of our frontiers, the merciless Indian Savages, whose known rule of warfare, is an undistinguished destruction of all ages, sexes and conditions.

In every stage of these Oppressions We have Petitioned for Redress in the most humble terms: Our repeated Petitions have been answered only by repeated injury. A Prince, whose character is thus marked by every act which may define a Tyrant, is unfit to be the ruler of a free People.

Nor have We been wanting in attentions to our British brethren. We have warned them from time to time of attempts by their legislature to extend an unwarrantable jurisdiction over us. We have reminded them of the circumstances of our emigration and settlement here. We have appealed to their native justice and magnanimity, and we have conjured them by the ties of our common kindred to disavow these usurpations, which would inevitably interrupt our connections and correspondence. They too have been deaf to the voice of justice and of consanguinity. We must, therefore, acquiesce in the necessity, which denounces our Separation, and hold them, as we hold the rest of mankind, Enemies in War, in Peace Friends.

We, therefore, the Representatives of the united States of America, in General Congress, Assembled, appealing to the Supreme Judge of the world for the rectitude of our intentions, do, in the Name, and by Authority of the good People of these Colonies, solemnly publish and declare, That these United Colonies are, and of Right ought to be Free and Independent States; that they are Absolved from all Allegiance to the British Crown, and that all political connection between them and the State of Great Britain, is and ought to be totally dissolved; and that as Free and Independent States, they have full Power to levy War, conclude Peace, contract Alliances, establish Commerce, and to do all other Acts and Things which Independent States may of right do. And for the support of this Declaration, with a firm reliance on the Protection of Divine Providence, we mutually pledge to each other our Lives, our Fortunes and our sacred Honor.

THE CONSTITUTION OF THE UNITED STATES

PREAMBLE

WE, the people of the United States, in order to form a more perfect Union, establish justice, insure domestic tranquility, provide for the common defence, promote the general welfare, and secure the blessings of liberty to ourselves and our posterity, do ordain and establish this Constitution for the United States of America.

LEGISLATURE

ARTICLE I. 1. All legislative powers herein granted, shall be vested in a Congress of the United States, which shall consist of a Senate and House of Representatives.

2. The House of Representatives shall be composed of members chosen every second year by the people of the several States; and the electors in each State shall have the qualifications requisite for electors of the most numerous branch of the State Legislature.

No person shall be a Representative who shall not have attained the age of twenty-five years, and been seven years a citizen of the United States, and who shall not, when elected, be an inhabitant of that State in which he shall be chosen.

Representatives and direct taxes shall be apportioned among the several States which may be included within this Union, according to their respective numbers, which shall be determined by adding to the whole number of free persons, including those bound to service for a term of years, and excluding Indians not taxed, three fifths of all other persons. The actual enumeration shall be made within three years after the first meeting of the Congress of the United States, and within every subsequent term of ten years, in such manner as they shall by law direct. The number of Representatives shall not exceed one for every thirty thousand, but each State shall have at least one Representative, and until such enumeration shall be made, the State of New Hampshire shall be entitled to choose three, Massachusetts eight, Rhode Island and Providence Plantations one, Connecticut five, New York six, New Jersey four, Pennsylvania eight, Delaware one, Maryland six, Virginia ten, North Carolina five, South Carolina five, and Georgia three.

When vacancies happen in the representation from any State, the Executive authority thereof shall issue writs of election to fill such vacancies.

The House of Representatives shall choose their Speaker and other officers; and shall have the sole power of impeachment.

3. The Senate of the United States shall be composed of two Senators from each State, chosen by the legislature thereof, for six years; and each Senator shall have one vote.

Immediately after they shall be assembled, in consequence of the first election, they shall be divided equally as may be into three classes. The seats of the Senators of the first class shall be vacated at the expiration of the second year, of the second class at the expiration of the fourth year, and of the third class at the expiration of the sixth year, so that one third may be chosen every second year; and if vacancies happen by resignation, or otherwise, during the recess of the legislature of any State, the Executive thereof may make temporary appointments until the next meeting of the legislature, which shall then fill such vacancies.

No person shall be a Senator who shall not have attained the age of thirty years, and been nine years a citizen of the United States, and who shall not, when elected, be an inhabitant of that State for which he shall be chosen.

The Vice President of the United States shall be President of the Senate, but shall have no vote, unless they be equally divided.

The Senate shall choose their other officers, and also a President *Pro Tempore*, in the absence of the Vice President, or when he shall exercise the office of President of the United States.

The Senate shall have the sole power to try all impeachments. When sitting for that purpose, they shall be on oath or affirmation. When the President of the United States is tried, the Chief Justice shall preside: and no person shall be convicted without the concurrence of two thirds of the members present.

Judgment in cases of impeachment shall not extend further than to removal from office, and disqualification to hold and enjoy any office of honour, trust or profit, under the United States; but the party convicted shall nevertheless be liable and subject to indictment, trial, judgment, and punishment according to law.

4. The times, places and manner of holding elections for Senators and Representatives, shall be prescribed in each State by the legislature thereof; but the Congress may at any time by law make or alter such regulations, except as to the places of choosing Senators.

The Congress shall assemble at least once in every year, and such meeting shall be on the first Monday in December, unless they shall by law appoint a different day.

5. Each House shall be the judge of the elections, returns, and qualifications of its own members, and a majority of each shall constitute a quorum to do business; but a smaller number may adjourn from day to day, and may be authorized to compel the attendance of absent members, in such manner, and under such penalties, as each House may provide.

Each House may determine the rules of its proceedings, punish its members for disorderly behaviour, and, with the concurrence of two thirds, expel a member.

Each House shall keep a journal of its proceedings, and from time to time publish the same, excepting such parts as may, in their judgment, require secrecy; and the yeas and nays of the members of either House on any question, shall, at the desire of one fifth of those present, be entered on the journal.

Neither House, during the session of Congress, shall, without the consent of the other, adjourn for more than three days, nor to any other place than that in which the two Houses shall be sitting.

6. The Senators and Representatives shall receive a compensation for their services, to be ascertained by law, and paid out of the Treasury of the United States. They shall, in all cases, except treason, felony, and breach of the peace, be privileged from arrest during their attendance at the session of their respective Houses, and in going to, and returning from, the same; and for any speech or debate in either House, they shall not be questioned in any other place.

No Senator or Representative shall, during the time for which he was elected, be appointed to any civil office under the authority of the United States, which shall have been created, or the emoluments whereof shall have been increased during such time; and no person holding any office under the United States, shall be a member of either House during his continuance in office.

7. All bills for raising revenue shall originate in the House of Representatives; but the Senate may propose or concur with amendments as on other bills.

Every bill which shall have passed the House of Representatives and the Senate, shall, before it become a law, be presented to the President of the United States; if he approve he shall sign it, but if not he shall return it, with his objections, to that House in which it shall have originated, who shall enter the objections at large on their journal, and proceed to reconsider it. If after such reconsideration two thirds of that House agree to pass the bill, it shall be sent, together with the objections, to the other House, by which it shall likewise be reconsidered, and if approved by two thirds of that House, it shall become a law. But in all cases the votes of both Houses shall be determined by yeas and nays, and the names of the persons voting for and against the bill shall be entered on the journal of each House respectively. If any bill shall not be returned by the President within ten days (Sundays excepted) after it shall have been presented to him, the same shall be a law in like manner as if he had signed it, unless the Congress by their adjournment prevent its return, in which case it shall not be a law.

Every order, resolution, or vote, to which the concurrence of the Senate and House of Representatives may be necessary (except on a question of adjournment), shall be presented to the President of the United States; and before the same shall take effect, shall be approved by him, or being disapproved by him, shall be re-passed by two thirds of the Senate and House of Representatives, according to the rules and limitations prescribed in the case of a bill.

8. The Congress shall have power

To lay and collect taxes, duties, imposts and excises, to pay the debts, and provide for the common defence and general welfare of the United States; but all duties, imposts, and excises shall be uniform throughout the United States:

To borrow money on the credit of the United States:

To regulate commerce with foreign nations, and among the several States, and with the Indian tribes:

To establish an uniform rule of naturalization, and uniform laws on the subject of bankruptcies throughout the United

States:

To coin money, regulate the value thereof, and of foreign coin, and fix the standard of weights and measures:

To provide for the punishment of counterfeiting the securities and current coin of the United States:

To establish post-offices and post-roads:

To promote the progress of science and useful arts, by securing, for limited times, to authors and inventors, the exclusive right to their respective writings and discoveries:

To constitute tribunals inferior to the Supreme Court:

To define and punish piracies and felonies committed on the high seas, and offences against the law of nations:

To declare war, grant letters of marque and reprisal, and make rules concerning captures on land and water:

To raise and support armies: but no appropriation of money to that use shall be for a longer term than two years:

To provide and maintain a navy:

To make rules for the government and regulation of the land and naval forces:

To provide for calling forth the militia to execute the laws of the Union, suppress insurrections and repel invasions:

To provide for organizing, arming, and disciplining the militia, and for governing such part of them as may be employed in the service of the United States, reserving to the States respectively, the appointment of the officers, and the authority of training the militia according to the discipline prescribed by Congress:

To exercise exclusive legislation, in all cases whatsoever, over such district (not exceeding ten miles square) as may, by cession of particular States, and the acceptance of Congress, become the seat of the government of the United States, and to exercise like authority over all places purchased by the consent of the legislature of the State in which the same shall be, for the erection of forts, magazines, arsenals, dock-yards, and other needful buildings. And,

To make all laws which shall be necessary and proper for carrying into execution the foregoing powers, and all other powers vested by this Constitution in the government of the United States, or in any department or officer thereof.

9. The migration or importation of such persons as any of the States now existing shall think proper to admit, shall not be prohibited by the Congress prior to the year one thousand eight hundred and eight; but a tax or duty may be imposed on such importation, not exceeding ten dollars for each person.

The privilege of the writ of *habeas corpus* shall not be suspended, unless when in cases of rebellion or invasion the public safety may require it.

No bill of attainder or *ex post facto* law shall be passed.

No capitation, or other direct tax, shall be laid, unless in proportion to the *census* or enumeration herein before directed to be taken.

No tax or duty shall be laid on articles exported from any State. No preference shall be given by any regulation of commerce or revenue to the ports of one State over those of another; nor shall vessels bound to, or from, one State be obliged to enter, clear, or pay duties in another.

No money shall be drawn from the treasury, but in consequence of appropriations made by law; and a regular statement and account of the receipts and expenditures of all public money shall be published from time to time.

No title of nobility shall be granted by the United States; and no person holding any office of profit or trust under them, shall, without the consent of the Congress, accept of any present, emolument, office, or title of any kind whatever, from any king, prince, or foreign state.

10. No State shall enter into any treaty, alliance, or confederation; grant letters of marque and reprisal; coin money; emit bills of credit; make any thing but gold and silver coin a tender in payment of debts; pass any bill of attainder, *ex post facto* law, or law impairing the obligation of contracts, or grant any title of nobility.

No State shall, without the consent of the Congress, lay any imposts or duties on imports or exports, except what may be absolutely necessary for executing its inspection laws; and the net produce of all duties and imposts, laid by any State on imports or exports, shall be for the use of the treasury of the United States: and all such laws shall be subject to the revision and control of the Congress. No state shall, without the consent of Congress, lay any duty of tonnage, keep troops, or ships of war, in time of peace, enter into any agreement or compact with another State, or with a foreign power, or engage in war, unless actually invaded, or in such imminent danger as will not admit of delay.

EXECUTIVE

ARTICLE II. 1. The executive power shall be vested in a President of the United States of America. He shall hold his office during the term of four years, and together with the Vice President, chosen for the same term, be elected as follows:

Each State shall appoint, in such manner as the legislature thereof may direct, a number of electors equal to the whole number of Senators and Representatives to which the State may be entitled in the Congress; but no Senator or Representative, or person holding an office of trust or profit under the United States, shall be appointed an elector.

The electors shall meet in their respective States, and vote by ballot for two persons, of whom one at least shall not be an inhabitant of the same State with themselves. And they shall make a list of all the persons voted for, and of the number of votes for each; which list they shall sign and certify, and transmit sealed to the seat of the government of the United States, directed to the President of the Senate. The President of the Senate shall, in the presence of the Senate and House of Representatives, open all the certificates, and the votes shall then be counted. The person having the greatest number of votes shall be the President, if such number be a majority of the whole number of electors appointed; and if there be more than one who have such majority, and have an equal number of votes, then the House of Representatives shall immediately choose by ballot one of them for President; and if no person have a majority, then from the five highest on the list the said House shall in like manner choose the President. But in choosing the President, the votes shall be taken by States, the representation from each State having one vote; a quorum for this purpose shall consist of a member or members from two thirds of the States, and a majority of all the States shall be necessary to a choice. In every case, after the choice of the President, the person having the greatest number of votes of the electors shall be the Vice President. But if there should remain two or more who have equal votes, the Senate shall choose from them by ballot the Vice President.

The Congress may determine the time of choosing the electors, and the day on which they shall give their votes; which day shall be the same throughout the United States.

No person except a natural born citizen, or a citizen of the United States, at the time of the adoption of this Constitution, shall be eligible to the office of President; neither shall any person be eligible to that office who shall not have attained the age of thirty-five years, and been fourteen years a resident within the United States.

In case of the removal of the President from office, or of his death, resignation, or inability to discharge the powers and duties of the said office, the same shall devolve on the Vice President, and the Congress may by law provide for the case of removal, death, resignation, or inability, both of the President and Vice President, declaring what officer shall then act as President, and such officer shall act accordingly until the disability be removed, or a President shall be elected.

The President shall at stated times, receive for his services, a compensation, which shall neither be increased nor diminished during the period for which he shall have been elected, and he shall not receive within that period any other emolument from the United States or any of them.

Before he enter on the execution of his office, he shall take the following oath or affirmation:

"I do solemnly swear (or affirm) that I will faithfully execute the office of President of the United States, and will, to the best of my ability, preserve, protect, and defend the Constitution of the United States."

2. The President shall be Commander-in-Chief of the Army and Navy of the United States, and of the militia of the several States, when called into the actual service of the United States; he may re-

quire the opinion, in writing, of the principal officer in each of the executive departments, upon any subject relating to the duties of their respective offices, and he shall have power to grant reprieves and pardons for offences against the United States, except in cases of impeachment.

He shall have power, by and with the advice and consent of the Senate, to make treaties, provided two thirds of the Senators present concur; and he shall nominate, and by and with the advice and consent of the Senate, shall appoint ambassadors, other public ministers and consuls, judges of the Supreme Court, and all other officers of the United States, whose appointments are not herein otherwise provided for, and which shall be established by law. But the Congress may by law vest the appointment of such inferior officers, as they think proper, in the President alone, in the courts of law, or in the heads of departments.

The President shall have power to fill up all vacancies that may happen during the recess of the Senate, by granting commissions which shall expire at the end of their session.

3. He shall, from time to time, give to the Congress information of the state of the Union, and recommend to their consideration such measures as he shall judge necessary and expedient. He may on extraordinary occasions, convene both Houses, or either of them; and in case of disagreement between them, with respect to the time of adjournment, he may adjourn them to such time as he shall think proper. He shall receive ambassadors and other public ministers. He shall take care that the laws be faithfully executed; and shall commission all the officers of the United States.

4. The President, Vice President, and all civil officers of the United States, shall be removed from office on impeachment for, and conviction of, treason, bribery, or other high crimes and misdemeanors.

JUDICIARY

ARTICLE III. 1. The judicial power of the United States shall be vested in one Supreme Court, and in such inferior courts as the Congress may, from time to time, ordain and establish. The judges, both of the Supreme and inferior courts, shall hold their offices during good behaviour; and shall, at stated times, receive for their services, a compensation, which shall not be diminished during their continuance in office.

2. The judicial power shall extend to all cases, in law and equity, arising under this Constitution, the laws of the United States, and treaties made, or which shall be made, under their authority; to all cases affecting ambassadors, other public ministers, and consuls; to all cases of admiralty and maritime jurisdiction; to controversies to which the United States shall be a party; to controversies between two or more States, between a State and citizens of another State, between citizens of different States, between citizens of the same State claiming lands under grants of different States, and between a State, or the citizens thereof, and foreign states, citizens or subjects.

In all cases affecting ambassadors, other public ministers and consuls, and those in which a State shall be party, the Supreme Court shall have original jurisdiction. In all the other cases before mentioned, the Supreme Court shall have appellate jurisdiction, both as to law and fact, with such exceptions, and under such regulations, as the Congress shall make.

The trial of all crimes, except in cases of impeachment, shall be by jury; and such trial shall be held in the State where the said crimes shall have been committed; but when not committed within any State, the trial shall be at such place or places as the Congress may by law have directed.

3. Treason against the United States, shall consist only in levying war against them, or in adhering to their enemies, giving them aid and comfort. No person shall be convicted of treason unless on the testimony of two witnesses to the same overt act, or on confession in open court.

The Congress shall have power to declare the punishment of treason, but no attainder of treason shall work corruption of blood, or forfeiture, except during the life of the person attained.

THE FEDERAL SYSTEM

ARTICLE IV. 1. Full faith and credit shall be given in each State to the public acts, records, and judicial proceedings of

185

every other State. And the Congress may by general laws prescribe the manner in which such acts, records, and proceedings shall be proved, and the effect thereof.

2. The citizens of each State shall be entitled to all privileges and immunities of citizens in the several States.

A person charged in any State with treason, felony, or other crime, who shall flee from justice, and be found in another State, shall, on demand of the executive authority of the State from which he fled, be delivered up to be removed to the State having jurisdiction of the crime.

No person held to service or labour in one State, under the laws thereof, escaping into another, shall, in consequence of any laws or regulation therein, be discharged from such service or labour, but shall be delivered up on claim of the party to whom such service or labour may be due.

3. New States may be admitted by the Congress into this Union; but no new State shall be formed or erected within the jurisdiction of any other State; nor any State be formed by the junction of two or more States, or parts of States, without the consent of the legislatures of the States concerned, as well as of Congress.

The Congress shall have power to dispose of and make all needful rules and regulations respecting the territory or other property belonging to the United States; and nothing in this Constitution shall be so construed as to prejudice any claims of the United States, or of any particular State.

4. The United States shall guarantee to every State in this Union a republican form of government, and shall protect each of them against invasion; and on application of the legislature, or of the executive (when the legislature cannot be convened), against domestic violence.

AMENDING THE CONSTITUTION

ARTICLE V. The Congress, whenever two thirds of both Houses shall deem it necessary, shall propose amendments to this Constitution, or, on the application of the legislatures of two thirds of the several States, shall call a convention for proposing amendments, which, in either case, shall be valid to all intents and purposes, as part of this Constitution, when ratified by the legislatures of three fourths of the several States, or by conventions in three fourths thereof, as the one or the other mode of ratification may be proposed by the Congress; provided that no amendment, which may be made prior to the year one thousand eight hundred and eight, shall in any manner affect the first and fourth clauses in the ninth section of the first article; and that no State, without its consent, shall be deprived of its equal suffrage in the Senate.

ARTICLE VI. All debts contracted, and engagements entered into, before the adoption of this Constitution, shall be as valid against the United States, under this Constitution, as under the confederation.

This Constitution, and the laws of the United States which shall be made in pursuance thereof, and all treaties made, or which shall be made, under the authority of the United States, shall be the supreme law of the land: and the judges, in every State, shall be bound thereby, any thing in the constitution or laws of any State to the contrary notwithstanding.

The Senators and Representatives before mentioned, and the members of the several State legislatures, and all executive and judicial officers, both of the United States and of the several States, shall be bound, by oath or affirmation, to support this Constitution; but no religious test shall ever be required as a qualification to any office or public trust under the United States.

ARTICLE VII. The ratification of the conventions of nine States, shall be sufficient for the establishment of this Constitution between the States so ratifying the same.

AMENDMENTS

(The first 10 amendments, adopted in 1791, are called the Bill of Rights)

ARTICLE I. Congress shall make no law respecting an establishment of religion, or prohibiting the free exercise thereof; or abridging the freedom of speech, or of the press; or the right of the people peaceably to assemble, and to petition the government for a redress of grievances.

ARTICLE II. A well regulated militia being necessary to the security of a free State, the right of the people to keep and bear arms shall not be infringed.

ARTICLE III. No soldier shall, in time of peace, be quartered in any house without the consent of the owner; nor in time of war, but in a manner to be prescribed by law.

ARTICLE IV. The right of the people to be secure in their persons, houses, papers, and effects, against unreasonable searches and seizures, shall not be violated; and no warrants shall issue, but upon probable cause, supported by oath or affirmation, and particularly describing the place to be searched, and the persons or things to be seized.

ARTICLE V. No person shall be held to answer for a capital or otherwise infamous crime, unless on a presentment or indictment of a grand jury, except in cases arising in the land or naval forces, or in the militia, when in actual service, in time of war or public danger; nor shall any person be subject for the same offence to be twice put in jeopardy of life or limb; nor shall be compelled, in any criminal case, to be witness against himself; nor be deprived of life, liberty, or property, without due process of law; nor shall private property be taken for public use without just compensation.

ARTICLE VI. In all criminal prosecutions the accused shall enjoy the right to a speedy and public trial, by an impartial jury of the State and district wherein the crime shall have been committed, which district shall have been previously ascertained by law, and to be informed of the nature and cause of the accusation; to be confronted with the witnesses against him; to have compulsory process for obtaining witnesses in his favour; and to have the assistance of counsel for his defence.

ARTICLE VII. In suits at common law, where the value of controversy shall exceed twenty dollars, the right of trial by jury shall be preserved; and no fact tried by a jury shall be otherwise re-examined in any court of the United States than according to the rules of the common law.

ARTICLE VIII. Excessive bail shall not be required, nor excessive fines imposed, nor cruel and unusual punishments inflicted.

ARTICLE IX. The enumeration in the Constitution of certain rights, shall not be construed to deny or disparage others retained by the people.

ARTICLE X. The powers not delegated to the United States by the Constitution, nor prohibited by it to the States, are reserved to the States respectively or to the people.

ARTICLE XI (1798). The Judicial power of the United States shall not be construed to extend to any suit in law or equity, commenced or prosecuted against one of the United States by Citizens or Subjects of any Foreign State.

ARTICLE XII (1804). The electors shall meet in their respective States, and vote by ballot for President and Vice-President, one of whom, at least shall not be an inhabitant of the same State with themselves; they shall name in their ballots the person voted for as President, and in distinct ballots the person voted for as Vice-President; and they shall make distinct lists of all persons voted for as President, and of all persons voted for as Vice-President, and of the number of votes for each, which list they shall sign and certify, and transmit sealed to the seat of the government of the United States, directed to the President of the Senate; the President of the Senate shall, in the presence of the Senate and House of Representatives, open all the certificates, and the votes shall then be counted: the person having the greatest number of votes for President shall be the President, if such number be a majority of the whole number of electors appointed; and if no person have such majority, then from the persons having the highest numbers, not exceeding three, on the list of those voted for as President, the House of Representatives shall choose immediately, by ballot, the President. But in choosing the President, the vote shall be taken by States, the representation from each State having one vote; a quorum for this purpose shall consist of a member or members from two thirds of the States, and a majority of all the States shall be necessary to a choice. And if the House of Representatives shall not choose a President whenever the right of choice shall devolve upon them, before the fourth day of March next following, then the Vice-President shall act as President, as in the case of the death or other constitutional disability of the President.

The person having the greatest number of votes as Vice-President shall be the

Vice-President, if such number be a majority of the whole number of electors appointed; and if no person have a majority, then from the two highest numbers on the list the Senate shall choose the Vice-President: a quorum for that purpose shall consist of two thirds of the whole number of Senators, and a majority of the whole number shall be necessary to a choice.

But no person constitutionally ineligible to the office of President shall be eligible to that of Vice-President of the United States.

ARTICLE XIII (1865). SECTION 1. Neither slavery nor involuntary servitude except as a punishment for crime whereof the party shall have been duly convicted, shall exist within the United States, or any place subject to their jurisdiction.

SECTION 2. Congress shall have power to enforce this article by appropriate legislation.

ARTICLE XIV (1868). SECTION 1. All persons born or naturalized in the United States, and subject to the jurisdiction thereof, are citizens of the United States and of the State wherein they reside. No State shall make or enforce any law which shall abridge the privileges or immunities of citizens of the United States; nor shall any State deprive any person of life, liberty, or property, without due process of law, nor deny to any person within its jurisdiction the equal protection of the laws.

SECTION 2. Representatives shall be apportioned among the several States according to their respective numbers, counting the whole number of persons in each State, excluding Indians not taxed. But when the right to vote at any election for the choice of electors for President and Vice-President of the United States, representatives in Congress, the executive and judicial officers of a State, or the members of the legislature thereof, is denied to any of the male inhabitants of such State, being twenty-one years of age, and citizens of the United States, or in anyway abridged, except for participation in rebellion or other crime, the basis of representation therein shall be reduced in the proportion which the number of such male citizens shall bear to the whole number of male citizens twenty-one years of age in such State.

SECTION 3. No person shall be a senator or representative in Congress, or elector of President and Vice-President, or hold any office, civil or military, under the United States, or under any State, who having previously taken an oath, as a member of Congress, or as an officer of the United States, or as a member of any State legislature, or as an executive or judicial officer of any State, to support the Constitution of the United States, shall have engaged in insurrection or rebellion against the same, or given aid or comfort to the enemies thereof. But Congress may by a vote of two-thirds of each house remove such disability.

SECTION 4. The validity of the public debt of the United States, authorized by law, including debts incurred for payment of pensions and bounties for services in suppressing insurrection or rebellion, shall not be questioned. But neither the United States nor any State shall assume or pay any debt or obligation incurred in aid of insurrection or rebellion against the United States, or any claim for the loss or emancipation of any slave; but all such debts, obligations, and claims shall be held illegal and void.

SECTION 5. The Congress shall have power to enforce, by appropriate legislation, the provisions of this article.

ARTICLE XV (1870). SECTION 1. The right of citizens of the United States to vote shall not be denied or abridged by the United States or by any State on account of race, color, or previous condition of servitude.

SECTION 2. The Congress shall have power to enforce this article by appropriate legislation.

ARTICLE XVI (1913). The Congress shall have power to lay and collect taxes on incomes, from whatever source derived, without apportionment among the several States, and without regard to any census or enumeration.

ARTICLE XVII (1913). The Senate of the United States shall be composed of two Senators from each State, elected by the people thereof, for six years; and each Senator shall have one vote. The electors in each State shall have the qualifications requisite for electors of the most numerous branch of the State legislatures.

When vacancies happen in the representation of any State in the Senate, the executive authority of such State shall issue writs of election to fill such vacancies: *Provided,* That the legislature of any State may empower the executive thereof to make temporary appointments until the people fill the vacancies by election as the legislature may direct.

This amendment shall not be so construed as to affect the election or term of any Senator chosen before it becomes valid as part of the Constitution.

ARTICLE XVIII (1919). SECTION 1. After one year from the ratification of this article the manufacture, sale, or transportation of intoxicating liquors within, the importation thereof into, or the exportation thereof from the United States and all territory subject to the jurisdiction thereof for beverage purposes is hereby prohibited.

SECTION 2. The Congress and the several States shall have concurrent power to enforce this article by appropriate legislation.

SECTION 3. This article shall be inoperative unless it shall have been ratified as an amendment to the Constitution by the legislatures of the several States, as provided in the Constitution, within seven years from the date of the submission hereof to the States by the Congress.

ARTICLE XIX (1920). The right of citizens of the United States to vote shall not be denied or abridged by the United States or by any State on account of sex.

Congress shall have power to enforce this article by appropriate legislation.

ARTICLE XX (1933). SECTION 1. The terms of the President and Vice President shall end at noon on the 20th day of January, and the terms of Senators and Representatives at noon on the 3rd day of January, of the years in which such terms would have ended if this article had not been ratified; and the terms of their successors shall then begin.

SECTION 2. The Congress shall assemble at least once in every year, and such meeting shall begin at noon on the 3rd day of January, unless they shall by law appoint a different day.

SECTION 3. If, at the time fixed for the beginning of the term of the President, the President elect shall have died, the Vice President elect shall become President. If a President shall not have been chosen before the time fixed for the beginning of his term, or if the President elect shall have failed to qualify, then the Vice President elect shall act as President until a President shall have qualified; and the Congress may by law provide for the case wherein neither a President elect nor a Vice President elect shall have qualified, declaring who shall then act as President, or the manner in which one who is to act shall be selected, and such person shall act accordingly until a President or Vice President shall have qualified.

SECTION 4. The Congress may by law provide for the case of the death of any of the persons from whom the House of Representatives may choose a President whenever the right choice shall have devolved upon them, and for the case of the death of any of the persons from whom the Senate may choose a Vice President whenever the right of choice shall have devolved upon them.

SECTION 5. Sections 1 and 2 shall take affect on the 15th day of October following the ratification of this article.

SECTION 6. This article shall be inoperative unless it shall have been ratified as an amendment to the Constitution by the legislatures of three-fourths of the several States within seven years from the date of its submission.

ARTICLE XXI (1933). SECTION 1. The eighteenth article of amendment to the Constitution of the United States is hereby repealed.

SECTION 2. The transportation or importation into any State, Territory, or possession of the United States for delivery or use therein of intoxicating liquors, in violation of the laws thereof, is hereby prohibited.

SECTION 3. This article shall be inoperative unless it shall have been ratified as an amendment to the Constitution by conventions in the several States, as provided in the Constitution, within seven years from the date of the submission hereof to the States by the Congress.

ARTICLE XXII (1951). SECTION 1. No person shall be elected to the office of the President more than twice, and no person who has held the office of President, or acted as President, for more than two years of a term to which some other person was elected President shall be elected to the office of the President more than once. But this Article shall not apply to any person holding the office of President when this Article was proposed by the Congress, and shall not prevent any person who may be holding the office of President, or acting as President, during the term within which this Article becomes operative from holding the office of President or acting as President during the remainder of such term.

ARTICLE XXIII (1961). SECTION 1. The District constituting the seat of Government of the United States shall appoint in such manner as the Congress may direct: A number of electors of President and Vice President equal to the whole number of Senators and Representatives in Congress to which the District would be entitled if it were a State, but in no event more than the least populous State; they shall be in addition to those appointed by the States, but they shall be considered, for the purposes of the election of President and Vice President, to be electors appointed by a State; and they shall meet in the District and perform such duties as provided by the twelfth article of amendment.

SECTION 2. The Congress shall have power to enforce this article by appropriate legislation.

ARTICLE XXIV (1964). SECTION 1. The right of citizens of the United States to vote in any primary or other election for President or Vice President, for electors for President or Vice President, or for Senator or Representatives in Congress, shall not be denied or abridged by the United States or any State by reason of failure to pay any poll tax or other tax.

SECTION 2. The Congress shall have the power to enforce this article by appropriate legislation.

ARTICLE XXV (1967). SECTION 1. In case of the removal of the President from office or his death or resignation, the Vice President shall become President.

SECTION 2. Whenever there is a vacancy in the office of the Vice President, the President shall nominate a Vice President who shall take office upon confirmation by a majority vote of both houses of Congress.

SECTION 3. Whenever the President transmits to the President Pro Tempore of the Senate and the Speaker of the House of Representatives his written declaration that he is unable to discharge the powers and duties of his office, and until he transmits to them a written declaration to the contrary, such powers and duties shall be discharged by the Vice President as Acting President.

SECTION 4. Whenever the Vice President and a majority of either the principal officers of the executive departments or of such other body as Congress may by law provide, transmit to the President Pro Tempore of the Senate and the Speaker of the House of Representatives their written declaration that the President is unable to discharge the powers and duties of his office the Vice President shall immediately assume the powers and duties of the office as Acting President.

Thereafter, when the President transmits to the President Pro Tempore of the Senate and the Speaker of the House of Representatives his written declaration that no inability exists, he shall resume the powers and duties of his office unless the Vice President and a majority of either the principal officers of the executive departments or of such other body as Congress may by law provide, transmit within four days to the President Pro Tempore of the Senate and the Speaker of the House of Representatives their written declaration that the President is unable to discharge the powers and duties of his office. Thereupon Congress shall decide the issue, assembling within 48 hours for that purpose if not in session. If the Congress, within 21 days after receipt of the latter written declaration, or, if Congress is not in session, within 21 days after Congress is required to assemble, determines by two-thirds vote of both houses that the President is unable to discharge the powers and duties of his office, the Vice President shall continue to discharge the same as Acting President; otherwise, the President shall resume the powers and duties of his office.

PHOTO AND ART CREDITS: 6, 10, The New York Public Library (2) • 11, The I.N. Phelps Stokes Collection, New York Public Library (2) • 12, (top) Culver Pictures; (bottom) A PHILADELPHIA ANABAPTIST IMMERSION, by Pavel Svinin, Courtesy of The Metropolitan Museum of Art, Rogers Fund, 1942 • 13, (top) Brown Brothers; (bottom) Culver Pictures • 14, (top) Culver Pictures; (bottom) Brown Brothers • 15, (left) Photoworld; (right & bottom) Brown Brothers • 16, The I.N. Phelps Stokes Collection, New York Public Library • 17, (top) THE MIDNIGHT RIDE OF PAUL REVERE, by Grant Wood, Courtesy of Associated American Artists and The Metropolitan Museum of Art, Arthur H. Hearn Fund, 1950; (bottom) The I.N. Phelps Stokes Collection, New York Public Library • 18, 22, The New York Public Library (2) • 25, Brown Brothers • 28, PATRICK HENRY, by Thomas Sully, Courtesy of The Colonial Williamsburg Collection • 32, THE BOSTONIANS PAYING THE EXCISE MAN, by P. Dawe, Courtesy of The Metropolitan Museum of Art, Bequest of Charles Allen Munn, 1924 • 35, 36, Culver Pictures (2) • 41, (top) THE HORSE AMERICA THROWING HIS MASTER, Courtesy of The Henry E. Huntington Library & Art Gallery; (bottom) The New York Public Library • 42, Frederic Lewis • 43, (top) THE BATTLE OF LEXINGTON, by John Baker, Courtesy of The Metropolitan Museum of Art, Bequest of Charles Allen Munn, 1924; (bottom) Culver Pictures • 44, (top) Culver Pictures; (bottom) Frederic Lewis • 45, 46, Culver Pictures (2) • 48, The New York Public Library • 52, The Library of Congress • 54, The New York Public Library • 58, Culver pictures • 60, The New York Public Library • 62, The Library of Congress • 64, Culver Pictures • 66, BENJAMIN FRANKLIN, by David Martin, Courtesy of The Pennsylvania Academy of Fine Arts • 70, Brown Brothers • 73, THOMAS JEFFERSON, by Mather Brown, Courtesy of The Smithsonian Institution • 76, Culver Pictures • 79, Brown Brothers • 80, The I.N. Phelps Stokes Collection, New York Public Library • 83, (top) A MILITIA MUSTER, by D. C. Johnston, Courtesy of The American Antiquarian Society; (bottom) Culver Pictures • 84, 88, 98, The Bettmann Archive (4) • 104, The I. N. Phelps Stokes Collection, New York Public Library (2) • 105, DANIEL BOONE, by James O. Lewis, Courtesy of The Missouri Historical Society • 106, (top) Courtesy of The Anne S. K. Brown Military Collection, Brown University Library; (bottom) The Smithsonian Institution • 107, (top) The Bettmann Archive; (bottom) SIOUX VILLAGE MOVING, by George Catlin, Courtesy of The New York Historical Society • 108, (top) The New York Public Library; (bottom) Courtesy of The Minnesota Historical Society • 109, (top) The I.N. Phelps Stokes Collection, New York Public Library; (bottom) The Bettmann Archive • 110, Photoworld (2) • 113, Courtesy of The Anne S.K. Brown Military Collection, Brown University Library • 117, ANDREW JACKSON, by Ralph Earl, Courtesy of The Smithsonian Institution • 121, Culver Pictures • 124, The Bettmann Archive • 127, Culver Pictures • 130, The New York Public Library • 134, Culver Pictures • 135, (top & right) The New York Public Library; (left) Culver Pictures • 136, (top) Culver Pictures; (bottom) The Schomburg Collection, New York Public Library • 137, (top) The Library of Congress; (bottom) Courtesy of The New York Historical Society • 138, The New York Public Library • 139, (left & right) Culver Pictures; (bottom) Brown Brothers • 140, (top) Underwood & Underwood; (bottom) The Schomburg Collection, New York Public Library • 141, The New York Public Library (3) • 142, Courtesy of the New York Historical Society • 143, (top) The New York Public Library; (bottom) The National Cotton Council • 144, 147, Culver Pictures (2) • 150, The New York Public Library • 155, Culver Pictures • 158, Courtesy of The Museum of Immigration • 160, (left & bottom) The New York Public Library; (right) The Bettmann Archive • 161, The Bettmann Archive (2) • 162, The New York Public Library (2) • 163, (top) The New York Public Library; (bottom) The Solomon Butcher Collection, Courtesy of The Nebraska State Historical Society • 164, 167, 169, The New York Public Library (3) • 170, Culver Pictures • 174, The Schomburg Collection, New York Public Library • Maps: Irmgard Lochner. *Cover by Mozelle Thompson.*